STEP-BY-STEP

50 Recipes for Kids to Cook

STEP-BY-STEP
50 Recipes for Kids to Cook

Judy Williams

Photography by David Jordan

SMITHMARK

For John and Chloe: years apart, but chips off the same block

This edition published in 1996 by
SMITHMARK Publishers, a division of US Media Holdings, Inc
16 East 32nd Street
New York NY 10016
USA

SMITHMARK books are available for bulk purchase for sales promotion
and for premium use. For details write or call
the Manager of Special Sales,
SMITHMARK Publishers,16 East 32nd Street
New York NY 10016; (212) 532-6600

© 1996 Anness Publishing Limited

Produced by Anness Publishing Limited
1 Boundary Row
London SE1 8HP

ISBN 1 8317 7279 4

Publisher: Joanna Lorenz
Senior Cookery Editor: Linda Fraser
Assistant Editor: Emma Brown
Designer: Lilian Lindblom
Food and props styling for photography: Judy Williams
Assistant Home Economist: Manisha Kanani

Printed and bound in Hong Kong

CONTENTS

Introduction   **6**

Techniques   **16**

Mix 'n' Match   **20**

SNAPPY SOUPS AND SNACKS   **22**

FAST AND FANTASTIC   **32**

FEASTS FOR FRIENDS   **46**

DAZZLING DESSERTS   **60**

BREEZY BAKES   **72**

DRINKS AND NIBBLES   **88**

Index   **96**

INTRODUCTION

Welcome to the wonderful world of food. We all need it, we all eat it and now you're going to find out how to cook it.

It would be easy never to prepare a meal again – supermarkets are stuffed with ready-made meals, but what's the fun in that? It's true you'll have to find time to shop and get everything ready, as well as doing the actual cooking, but the thrill of serving and eating something you have made with your own clean hands is fantastic.

This book is split into sections. The first part is the bossy part, which tells you what to do and what not to do to be safe in the kitchen. Then there's lots of information about equipment and about words used in cooking that you might not understand. After that it's onto the exciting part – choosing what to cook. Some recipes are simple and these are a good place to start if you haven't done any cooking before. There are also lots of recipes that seem more difficult but, in fact, just take a bit longer.

All basic cooking techniques have been included in one recipe or another, so you will learn lots of useful skills that can be swapped around as you get more experienced. These skills may be useful for some school tests, and will certainly be invaluable when you leave home and have to feed yourself. You'll probably be feeding your friends as well, once they learn of your talents!

As well as stacks of snacks and super meals, there are plenty of desserts, cakes and cookies to choose from, with chocolate included in as many as possible!

Turning It On

The kitchen is full of things that could be very dangerous, such as electrical sockets, hot ovens and stovetops, fast-moving and sharp-bladed equipment and hot pans. So it's very important that you take as much care as possible.

Washing up is the most boring part about cooking, so keep it to a minimum and wash up as much as possible as you go along. Or stack the dishwasher, of course, but in any case, try to leave the room tidy or your days in the kitchen may be numbered!

Is the work surface too high? Making pastry or cakes means working in a mixing bowl and it might be hard to get your hands right in there. Put the bowl on the kitchen table or stand it in the empty sink instead, as both these places are much lower than a kitchen work surface.

Too hot to handle? Always use oven mitts or a thickly folded, dry dish towel (wet ones let the heat straight through) to lift things in and out of the oven. Keep saucepan handles turned away from any heat source and check they aren't hot, before trying to lift the pan.

Water, water everywhere: some recipes call for hot liquids and foods to be drained or poured into something else. Please do this very carefully.

Don't overfill the pan and, if it's too heavy or you aren't sure you can manage, ask a grown-up for some help.

A helping hand? Watch out for younger members of the family who want to help, especially if the oven is hot or you are frying things. If they really won't go away, find them something simple to do, such as arranging tomatoes in a bowl, or greasing cake pans; give them a small piece of pastry or dough to play with. Pets can also be a hazard: they creep in and try to trip you up, so bear them in mind.

Whoops: any wet spills on the floor, especially oil, should be wiped up at once. Use hot, soapy water and then dry the area well so the floor doesn't become a skating rink.

All this is not really complicated: it's a matter of being careful and sensible and thinking about what you are doing. Remember that most accidents happen in the home: make sure you aren't one of them!

Tie long hair back while you are cooking – then it can't get caught on equipment, will keep away from flames and won't become an extra ingredient in your recipe!

Always wash your hands – not just when you begin to cook but as you handle different ingredients. Garlic-flavored cakes are disgusting and no one finds gray pastry attractive!

Water and electricity don't mix, so dry your hands before touching any sockets or plugging in machinery. Turn off before pulling out the plug.

Read through the recipe before you start. Have everything ready: panic causes problems! Protect your clothes: wear an apron or old shirt if you are a messy cook, and remember to roll up those sleeves first!

Equipment

All cooking jobs in the kitchen need a tool of some sort, although a few basic ones can do most jobs. The biggest one is the stove.

Stoves

Almost all stoves in the U.S. are powered by electricity or gas; you will most likely have one of these. Temperature is measured in Fahrenheit (F°) and is the same for electricity and gas. The only differences will be between individual stoves. If possible get someone who has used the stove a lot to give you hints on how accurately it heats.

The oven is hottest on the top shelf, although most things are best cooked on the middle one. If two baking trays are going in at the same time, the one nearer the top of the oven will be cooked more quickly.

When the recipe says to preheat the oven, remember it will take about 10 minutes to reach the specified temperature; if you put the food in before the oven is hot enough, it will take longer to cook and some food will not cook correctly.

Stoves usually have three different cooking places – the oven, the broiler and the stovetop.

The oven cooks large items of food slowly and evenly, with the minimum of attention.

The broiler cooks quickly, so broiled food must be smaller and thinner or the outside will burn before the middle is properly cooked (even though there is a temperature control).

You have to keep a close watch on the food and it will need to be turned often.

The stovetop is the name for the four burners or hot plates on the top of the oven: in some kitchens, the stovetop is separate from the oven. You use saucepans or frying pans to cook food on the stovetop. Control-knobs can be turned up to cook things quickly, or turned down low to cook more slowly.

Timers

Modern stoves often have a built-in timer, rather like an alarm clock. Set it to the recommended cooking time and it makes a horrible buzzing noise that reminds you to take the food out.

Microwave Ovens

These machines make all the water molecules in food jump around and heat up, which cooks food quickly. They are brilliant at thawing frozen food, re-heating cooked food, melting chocolate and baking potatoes. But most of them can't turn food brown or cook large amounts of anything.

Safety First for Microwave Ovens

Never put any foil, metal dishes or plates with metallic edges in microwaves, and follow recipe instructions carefully.

The standing time mentioned at the end of lots of microwave recipes is part of the cooking, so don't be tempted to skip it.

Safety First for Ovens and Stovetops

When the oven is working, obviously the door becomes very hot and this can be dangerous if you have younger brothers and sisters who want to help. If your stove is new it may have a stay-cool door, which is much safer. Otherwise, watch out for this.

Energy Tips for Ovens and Stovetops

Save energy and cut fuel bills:
- Only use as much water as you need in pans and kettles.
- Put lids on saucepans and reduce the heat once the contents have come to a boil.
- Flames that lick up the sides of a pan are wasting energy, so adjust the flame.
- Steam a second vegetable in a colander over the potatoes.
- Try to cook more than one thing in the oven at a time.

Working Tools

There are probably lots of weird and wonderful things in the kitchen cabinets and drawers, here's a guide to help you find out what they do.

colander

nutmeg grater

baking tray

Food Processors

This is actually a giant blender, with a large bowl and, usually, lots of attachments. The metal chopping blade is the one we use most, it's best with dry ingredients like vegetables and pastry. The plastic blade is for batters and cakes. Some processors also have grating blades and slicing plates.

Electric Beaters

A beater's main function is to beat in air and make the mixture bigger and thicker, as for cream and cake mixtures. But a beater can also blend things together and make them smooth, such as sauces, eggs or drinks.

Blenders

These usually attach to an electric beater motor or a food processor and are tall and deep, with blades at the bottom. Ideal for turning things into liquid such as fruit for sauces, soups and milkshakes. Hand-held blenders are smaller and can be used in a small bowl or mug.

Safety First for Beaters, Blenders and Processors

Never put your hand in the processor to move something while it is plugged in. And keep small fingers away from beaters while they are whizzing round. Treat all electrical equipment very carefully and unplug everything before you fiddle around with blades or anything else.

Chopping Boards

Lots of people use the same board for all their preparation, but it's much more hygienic to use a different one for each type of job. It is possible to buy boards with colored handles, so the same one is always used for the same job. A wooden board is best for cutting bread. Scrub boards well after use.

Graters

A pyramid- or box-shaped grater is the most useful type. Each side has a different grating surface, made up of small, curved, raised blades. Use the coarsest one for vegetables and cheese and the finer sides for grating orange and lemon rind. Stand the grater on a flat surface while you use it and the grated food collects inside the pyramid. Scrub well with a brush after use. There are also very small graters, for whole nutmegs.

Measuring Equipment

In the U.S. most kitchen recipe measurements are given in spoons and cups as we weigh by volume, not weight. Ounces (oz) and pounds (lb) are sometimes used in recipes and are also to be found on supermarket packages.

Liquid measurements are always by volume. The thing to remember is that a dry ounce measures weight and a wet ounce measures volume; the two aren't necessarily the same.

Small amounts of dry and wet ingredients are often measured in teaspoons (tsp) and tablespoons (tbsp); note that:

3 tsp = 1 tbsp
2 tbsp = 1 oz/⅛ cup
4 tbsp = ¼ cup
8 tbsp = ½ cup

The spoon should be level and full, not heaped.

Bowls

Mixing bowls come in lots of sizes and the most useful are made from heatproof glass or stainless steel. Use large ones for pastry, bread-making and beating egg whites and smaller ones for smaller quantities, such as beating eggs, mixing dips and melting chocolate.

Pans

Saucepans and frying pans can be made from different metals; some are even glass! The most popular are aluminum pans and stainless steel ones. Pans need to have a thick bottom to keep food from sticking.

cake pan

saucepans

saucepan

springform
cake pans

frying pan

wire cooling
rack

grater

muffin
pan

whisks

measuring cups

weighing scales

food processor

mixing bowls

measuring
spoons

chopping boards

measuring cup

electric blender

Small Tools

Can opener
The two "arms" are squeezed together, so the blades at the top pierce the can. Turn the handle around and around and the top of the can will come off.

Canelle knife
This is rather like a zester, but cuts a thicker strip of rind.

Corer
Looks rather like a potato peeler but has a tube of metal that is pushed through the center of an apple to pull out the core.

Garlic press
Squashes the garlic cloves through small holes ready for cooking; you need a brush with stiff bristles to poke through the holes to get it clean again.

Hand beaters
A spring beater is most effective, good for cream or eggs.

Kitchen scissors
Used for cutting things like bacon, but also perfect for snipping herbs.

Knives
I am sure you know that knives must be used very carefully, but it's easy to get careless. Don't use a huge bread knife to peel an apple: pick the right size for the right job and try not to be distracted. No conducting with the carving knife!

You will only need five basic knives to do most jobs in this book. *Paring knife*, with a 3in blade, for peeling and trimming fruit and vegetables. *Cook's knife*, with a 6in blade, for general slicing. *Chopping knife*, with an 8in blade, for chopping and slicing. *Bread knife*, with a 10in blade with serrated edge, for cutting bread. *Metal spatula*, with a long, flexible blade, for lifting and spreading. All knives get blunt after a while and should be sharpened carefully, using a special knife-sharpening gadget.

Ladle
A large, deep spoon, used mainly for serving soup.

Lemon squeezer
The cut side of a halved citrus fruit is pressed down and squeezed over the central "spike". The juice runs down and collects in the base, ready for pouring.

Pastry bag and nozzles
Big ones are best for cookie mixes. A nozzle is dropped into the bag until it pokes out of the other end. Small ones are better for piping icing and frosting.

Pastry brush
For brushing egg onto pastry; also good for brushing sauces or oil over meat or vegetables.

Pastry wheel
Used for making a decoratively cut edge for pastry or ravioli.

Potato peeler
Some have fixed peeler blades with wooden handles; other have a more mobile blade and this can make peeling easier.

Rolling pin
Usually wooden, although marble ones keep pastry cool.

Rubber spatula
A wooden handle with a flexible blade, it's very good at getting mixing bowls clean.

Skewers
Metal or wooden ones are used for kebabs; metal ones are also good for pushing into cakes, to see if they're cooked.

Slotted spoon
For lifting and draining food.

Spatula
For lifting and turning burgers, fish, or even eggs!

Strainers
These come in various sizes. A small one is ideal for sifting confectioner's sugar over cakes. Larger ones are used for sifting flour and draining vegetables.

Tongs
Used for turning things over.

Wooden spoons
Come in various lengths. Short ones are better for beating cake mixtures and chocolate, but ones with longer handles are better for cooking on the stovetop, as your hand is further from the heat.

Zester
A small tool with five tiny round blades at the end. When it is dragged across an orange or lemon, it removes long thin shreds of rind that can be used in a recipe or as a garnish.

lemon

hand beater

pastry bag and nozz

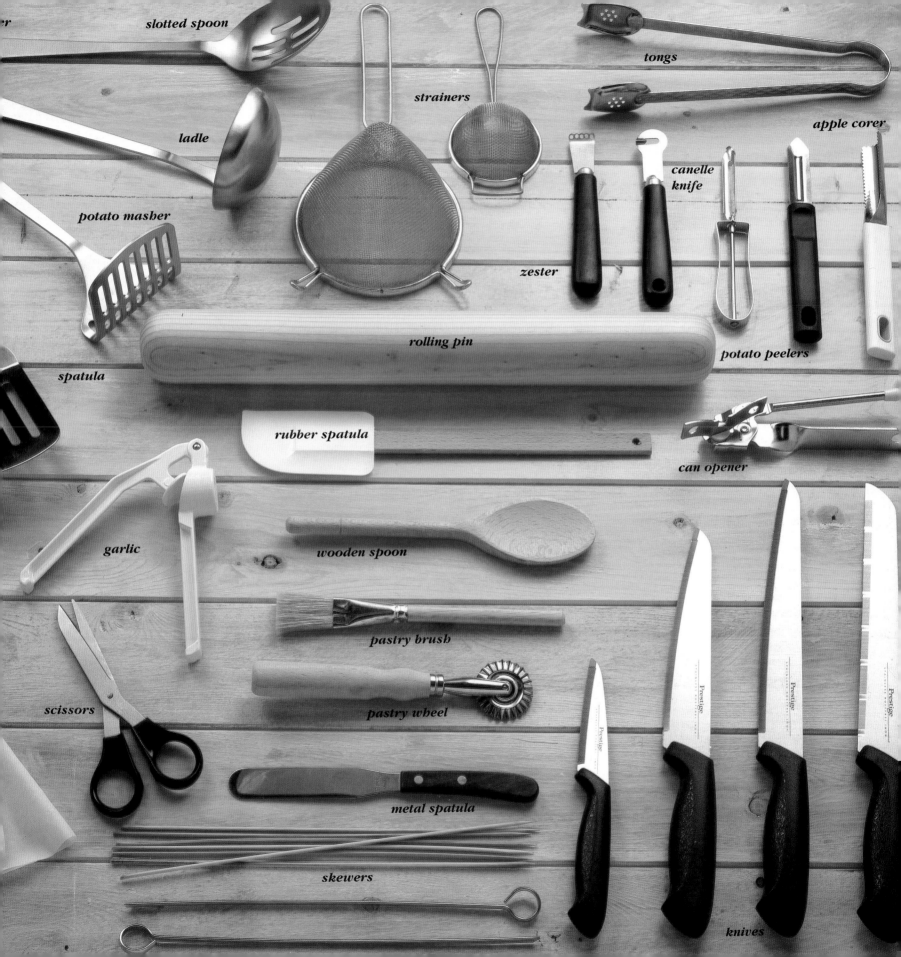

slotted spoon

tongs

strainers

ladle

apple corer

canelle
knife

potato masher

zester

rolling pin

potato peelers

spatula

rubber spatula

can opener

garlic

wooden spoon

pastry brush

scissors

pastry wheel

metal spatula

skewers

knives

A–Z of Cooking Terms

Sometimes cooking seems like a foreign language, with lots of words you aren't sure about. Hopefully this A–Z guide will explain what most of the words mean and then you'll be ready to get going in the kitchen.

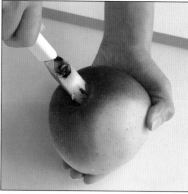

Coring

Dredging

Bake
To cook in the oven, in dry heat, at a set temperature.

Barbecue
A method of cooking food over glowing charcoal, which gives food a smoky taste.

Baste
To spoon fat and cooking juices over meat while cooking, to keep the meat tender and moist.

Blend
To mix ingredients evenly. Also used to describe the action of a blender.

Boil
A liquid is boiling when the edges are rolling over and large bubbles are heaving on the surface. This is called a rolling boil and that's how it looks. Usually, at this point, the heat is turned down and the liquid starts to simmer. There aren't many things that are cooked at a rolling boil, except raw beans, pasta and caramel. The action would be too fierce for most vegetables.

Bone
To remove bones from meat, fish or poultry.

Brown
Meat and vegetables are often browned at the start of a recipe, to give a good, even color and seal in the flavor. The food is turned over frequently, usually in hot fat.

Core
To cut out the tough central part and seeds of a fruit. This is easiest with a corer. Push it into the apple, over the stalk, and twist. Pull the corer out and the core will come out as well.

Cream
To beat fat (usually butter or margarine) and sugar together until they are light and fluffy, when making cakes.

Dredge
To cover something with an even layer of flour or sugar, for instance, dredging brownies with confectioner's sugar.

Dust
To sprinkle food lightly with flour or sugar – like dusting a loaf with flour before baking.

Flake
To divide cooked fish into its natural flakes after peeling away any skin and bones.

Fold in
To add something to a mixture very gently, so as not to break up all the air bubbles – as when folding beaten egg white into soufflés, and flour into sponge cakes – so the mixture stays light and fluffy.

Fry
To cook food in hot fat or oil, usually to get a crisp, browned surface on the outside.

Garnish
To decorate savory food with herbs, chopped vegetables or fruit, to make it look attractive before serving.

Glaze
Brushing pastry or bread with egg or milk will make it shiny and look more attractive.

Grate
To shred into tiny strips using a grater (see also page 18).

Grease
Brushing cooking pans or trays with a little oil or a margarine wrapper helps to keep food from sticking while it cooks.

Knead
To work dough until it is smooth and elastic (stretchy).

Line a pan
Putting a paper lining inside the pan, to keep food from sticking.

Marinade
A flavored liquid, usually tart and using oil, lemon juice or wine. Meat is sometimes soaked in a marinade to make it more tender and tasty.

Marinate
To leave meat, fish or poultry in a marinade for a while.

Parboil
To start cooking food, like potatoes, in boiling water, before moving onto the next stage of the cooking process, such as roasting. Parboiling speeds up the roasting time.

Pipe
To force food from a pastry bag through a nozzle into decorative shapes. Large nozzles might be used for cookies, cream or mashed potato and smaller ones for icing.

Folding in

Garnishing

Working in

Zesting

Poach

To cook food gently in simmering, not boiling, water.

Purée

To turn soft, solid food into a smoother thicker food – for example, lumpy vegetable soup can be puréed in a blender to make it smooth.

Roast

To cook uncovered in the oven by dry heat.

Roux

Equal quantities of butter or margarine and all-purpose flour are cooked together, to make the thickening for a white sauce. The fat is melted in a saucepan and then the flour mixed in. A roux should be cooked gently for 1–2 minutes before the liquid, usually milk, is added.

Rub or work in

To mix the fat into the flour when making pastry, crumble topping and some cakes. Use your fingertips to lift lumps of fat and flour and work them together to break the fat into smaller and smaller pieces, until it looks like bread crumbs. Hold your fingers high over the bowl to mix air into the mixture at the same time. A pastry blender can also be used.

Seasoning

Seasoning usually means to add salt and pepper to savory dishes, to heighten the flavor. Other aromatic ingredients added in small quantities, such as herbs, or chili powder could also be called seasonings.

Shallow-fry

To cook food in a thin layer of oil, so it browns and crisps on the outside.

Sift

To shake dry foods through a strainer to remove any lumps. Or push food through the strainer with a wooden spoon to purée it, instead of using a blender or food processor.

Simmer

To reduce the heat once the liquid has come to a boil so the liquid still bubbles lightly and is not completely calm.

Snipping

Using kitchen scissors to cut things in small pieces, rather than chopping them. A good way to cut up bacon, herbs, dried fruits and bread.

Stir-fry

A fast way to cook food over a high heat in very little oil. Food must be cut into small even-size pieces and kept moving all the time, to stop it burning. This is traditionally done in a wok, but a large, deep frying-pan can also be used.

Stock

A tasty liquid that is used to make soups and cook rice. Vegetable trimmings and bones can be boiled in water and the water turns to stock as it picks up the flavor. It is quicker and easier to use bouillon cubes. They come in lots of different flavors, so choose the one that suits your recipe best, for example, use chicken bouillon cubes for chicken dishes. Usually one bouillon cube is enough to flavor 2½ cups of water, but check the package instructions first.

Thicken

To give thinner sauces and gravies more body, by adding a thickening agent, such as cornstarch. Mix it with a little water and pour it into the boiling liquid, stirring all the time (to keep it from going lumpy), until it comes back to a boil and the liquid starts to thicken.

Whisk or beat

To mix air into egg whites or yolks. Beaten egg whites go through several different stages as they thicken, so check the recipe carefully. "Soft peaks" means the egg white will stand in peaks but the tops will flop over. "Stiff peaks" means the peaks will not flop over; finally they become stiff and look dry.

Zest

To remove the colored part of the rind of citrus fruit (lemons, oranges, etc.). Use a fine grater or a zester (see page 12).

TECHNIQUES

Preparing ingredients is easy when you follow
these step-by-step instructions.

Preparing Onions

Keeping the onions a similar size means they all
cook at the same time, but we don't want any
sliced fingertips, so be careful!

1 Cut the onion in half with the skin
still on. Lie the cut side flat on a board.
Trim off both ends. Peel off the skin.

2 Make several parallel cuts
lengthwise (from trimmed end to end),
but not cutting right to one end.

3 Make cuts at right angles to the first
ones, at the same distance apart. The
onion will be finely chopped. Finally,
chop the end.

COOK'S TIP
When an onion is described as
"sliced", cut down through each
half to make vertical slices.

Preparing Carrots

Although they are often just sliced in circles,
carrots can look much more attractive cut in a
different way.

1 Peel the carrot, using this quick method with a swivel peeler, and trim the ends.

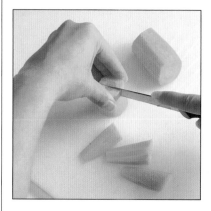

2 Cut the carrot into short lengths
and then into thin slices, lengthwise.
You will need a sharp knife for this job,
so be careful.

3 Cut each thin slice into fine strips,
about the size of matchsticks.

COOK'S TIP
Use tiny cutters to stamp out
shapes from the thin carrot slices,
to garnish soup or salads.

Grating Fresh Ginger

Ground ginger is fine in cakes, but when it comes to a stir-fry, it has to be fresh.

1 The size is often given as a measurement, because the "root" is long and knobbly and difficult to weigh accurately. Break off roughly the size you need.

2 Use a peeler, or sharp knife if the ginger is really lumpy, and cut away the tough outer layer.

3 Grate on the coarsest side of the grater and use the strips for your recipe. Don't use any hard or stringy bits of ginger.

COOK'S TIP
Fresh ginger has a strong, spicy, flavor, so don't put in too much if you don't like hot food.

Grating Lemon Rind and Squeezing Lemon Juice

Recipes sometimes call for the grated rind and juice of a lemon.

1 Rinse the lemon and rub it up and down the fine grating side of the grater, until the yellow rind has come off. Stop grating once the white pith underneath shows through. Keep moving the grater around the lemon, until all the yellow rind is off. Some rind will collect inside the grater.

 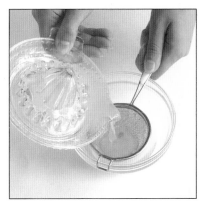

2 Cut the lemon in half, press one half down on to the pointed part of the squeezer and twist. Keep pressing and twisting and the juice will come out of the lemon. The larger seeds all collect at the base and are held back by the glass "teeth."

3 Smaller seeds might sneak through. Either fish them out with a spoon or your fingers, or pour the juice through a small strainer before adding it to the mixture.

COOK'S TIP
Oranges and limes may be grated and squeezed the same way.

Separating Eggs

Meringues and some sauces call for just egg whites, so they must be separated from the yolk.

1 Break the egg onto a saucer.

2 Stand an egg cup over the yolk and hold it firmly in place, taking care not to puncture the yolk.

3 Hold the saucer over the mixing bowl and let the egg white slide in, hanging on to the egg cup. The yolk will be left on the saucer.

COOK'S TIP
The yolk may be needed for glazing, so check the recipe before you throw it away.

Grating

The most popular grater is the pyramid or box type, which has different-sized blades for grating.

1 The very fine side is for grating whole nutmeg. Hold the nutmeg in one hand and rub it up and down the grater. Sometimes, it is easier to do this directly over the food.

2 The finer blades are best for citrus fruits. The blades only work downwards and you might need to brush out some of the rind from the inside with a dry pastry brush.

3 The coarsest side is best for cheese, fruit and vegetables. The blades work when you press downwards and the food will collect inside the grater.

COOK'S TIP
The jagged punched holes down one side of the grater are ideal for making breadcrumbs.

Whipping Cream

Cream can be bought in various thicknesses, so choose heavy cream, if you need it to be thick for your recipe. Don't try whipping light cream!

1 Pour the cream into a bowl and use an electric mixer to whip the cream. Keep the electric mixer moving around as you whisk.

2 A hand-held whisk works well but it takes much longer and makes your arm tired! The cream will first reach a soft and floppy stage, then get thicker and thicker the more you whisk.

3 Once whisk lines are left in the cream and it looks fairly stiff, it's time to stop whipping. Cream will start to look like mashed potato as it curdles and reaches the over-whipped stage.

Lining a Pan

Keep food, mainly cakes, from sticking to the pan by lining the pan with wax paper.

1 Stand the pan on the paper and draw around the bottom. Cut out the shape, just inside the line.

2 Wrap a strip of paper around the outside of the pan and cut it 2in longer and ½in wider than the pan.

3 Fold one long edge over by 1in. Make diagonal cuts at regular intervals up to the fold. Grease the pan lightly, to help the paper stick to it. Put the long strip inside the pan, around the edges, so the fringed paper sits on the bottom. Lie the round piece of paper over the top.

COOK'S TIP
If you only need to line the bottom of a pan, and not the sides as well; just follow step 1.

Mix 'n' Match

Most dishes need something to go with them, to turn them into a complete meal.
Here are some quick and easy ideas for accompaniments.

Making Mashed Potatoes

Check the labeling on the packages to see which potatoes are good for mashing; or you could ask your grocer.

Serves 4

INGREDIENTS
1lb potatoes, peeled and
    quartered
2 tbsp butter
2 tbsp milk or cream
salt and pepper

1 Cook the potatoes in a pan with enough room to mash them. Cover with water, add a little salt and bring the water to a boil. Turn down the heat and simmer for 20–25 minutes. The potatoes should feel tender and fall off a sharp knife when cooked.

Cook's Tip
Add two crushed cloves of garlic or a handful of chopped fresh herbs, to make a real change.

2 Drain the potatoes in a colander and return them to the pan. Add the butter, milk or cream and black pepper and use a potato masher to squash them and flatten all the lumps. Add more milk if you like them really soft.

Cooking Rice

Measure rice in a cup, by volume rather than by weight, for best results.

Serves 2

INGREDIENTS
2 tsp oil
⅔ cup long grain white rice
1¾ cups boiling water or stock
salt

Cook's Tip
Instant or minute rices will not take as long; check cooking times on the package.

1 Heat the oil in a saucepan and add the rice. Stir to coat all the grains with the oil.

2 Pour on the boiling water or stock, add a little salt and stir once before putting on the lid. Turn down the heat so the liquid is just simmering gently and walk away. Leave it alone for 15 minutes.

3 Lift the lid carefully (away from you) and check whether the rice is tender and that the liquid has almost gone. Fluff up the grains of rice with a fork and serve immediately.

Cooking Pasta

Pasta comes in lots of different shapes, sizes and colors. Green pasta has spinach in it, red pasta has tomato and brown pasta is made from wholewheat flour. Egg pasta has extra eggs in the dough. Allow about 4oz dried pasta per person if it is the main ingredient, and a little less if it is to accompany a meal, although this may vary according to how hungry you are!

Serves 4

INGREDIENTS
12 oz–1 lb dried pasta
salt

COOK'S TIP
Fresh pasta is also available, but its cooking times are shorter – check package instructions

1 Bring a large saucepan of water to a boil. Add a little salt. Add the pasta to the pan, a little at a time, so that the water stays at a rolling boil.

2 Cook for 8–12 minutes, depending on what type of pasta you are using – spaghetti will not take as long as the thicker penne pasta. It should be *al dente* when cooked, which means it still has some firmness to it and isn't completely soft and soggy.

3 Drain the pasta well in a colander and tip it back to the pan. Pour a sauce over or toss in a little melted butter.

Making Salad Dressing

Green or mixed salads add crunch and freshness to heavy, meaty meals like lasagne or barbecued ribs, but they are bland and boring without a dressing like this one.

Serves 4

INGREDIENTS
1 tbsp white wine vinegar
2 tsp coarse-grain mustard
salt
freshly ground black pepper
2 tbsp oil

COOK'S TIP
Mix 2 tbsp oil with 1 tbsp lemon juice, for a tangier dressing. Add chopped fresh herbs for extra flavor.

1 Put the vinegar and mustard in a bowl or jug. Beat well, then add a little salt and pepper.

2 Add the oil slowly, about 1tsp at a time, beating constantly. Pour the dressing over the salad just before serving so that the lettuce stays crisp. Use two spoons to toss the salad and coat it with the dressing.

Skinny Dips

Baking potatoes in disguise, with a dip
to scoop out.

Serves 4

Ingredients
8 large potatoes, scrubbed
2–3 tbsp oil
6 tbsp mayonnaise
2 tbsp plain yogurt
1 tsp curry paste
2 tbsp coarsely chopped
  fresh cilantro
salt

curry paste

potatoes

mayonnaise

fresh cilantro

natural yogurt

1 Preheat the oven to 375°F. Arrange the potatoes in a roasting pan, prick them all over with a fork and cook for 45 minutes, or until tender. Let them cool slightly.

2 Carefully cut each potato into quarters lengthwise, holding it with a clean dish towel if it's still a bit hot.

3 Scoop out some of the center with a knife or spoon and put the skins back in the roasting pan. Save the cooked potato for making fish cakes.

4 Brush the skins with oil and sprinkle with salt before putting them back in the oven. Cook for another 30–40 minutes, until they are crisp and brown, brushing them occasionally with oil.

5 Meanwhile, put the mayonnaise, yogurt, curry paste and 1 tbsp cilantro in a small bowl and mix together well. Let stand for 30–40 minutes for the flavor to develop.

6 Put the dip in a clean bowl and arrange the skins around the edge. Serve hot, sprinkled with the remaining cilantro.

Cook's tip

If there is just one of you, prick one large potato all over with a fork and microwave on HIGH for 6–8 minutes, until tender. Scoop out the center, brush with oil and broil until browned.

Pile-it-High Mushrooms

Ideal for you vegetarians out there, this speedy snack is great on its own, or on toast or with crusty bread. If you're really starving, add a few shrimp crackers.

Serves 4

INGREDIENTS
4 tbsp butter or corn oil
2 garlic cloves, peeled and
   crushed
4 large flat mushrooms, peeled
   or wiped
1in piece fresh ginger, grated
4 scallions, cut in 1in pieces
1 carrot, cut in matchsticks
6 baby corn, quartered
   lengthwise
3 oz thin green beans, halved
2 tbsp soy sauce
4 oz bean sprouts, rinsed
   and drained

thin green beans
baby corn
scallions
fresh ginger
garlic
carrot
soy sauce
butter
flat mushrooms
bean sprouts

1 Melt the butter or oil in a large frying pan and fry the garlic until it has softened slightly. Put the mushrooms in the pan and fry gently for 8–10 minutes, turning once or twice, until tender. Lift out the mushrooms, place in a dish and cover to keep them hot.

2 Turn up the heat and add the ginger, scallions, carrot, corn and beans to the pan and stir-fry for 2 minutes.

3 Add the soy sauce and bean sprouts and cook for 1 minute more. Put each mushroom on a plate and top with the stir-fried vegetables. Serve immediately.

Nutty Chicken Kebabs

A tasty Thai appetizer that's quick to make and uses everyone's favorite spread in the dip.

Serves 4

INGREDIENTS
2 tbsp oil
1 tbsp lemon juice
1 lb boneless, skinless chicken
   breasts, cut in small cubes,
   to fit on skewers

FOR THE DIP
1 tsp chili powder
5 tbsp water
1 tbsp oil
1 small onion, grated
1 garlic clove, peeled and
   crushed
2 tbsp lemon juice
4 tbsp crunchy peanut butter
1 tsp salt
1 tsp ground coriander
sliced cucumber and lemon
   wedges, to serve

lemon juice

crunchy peanut butter

onion

oil

chili powder

chicken

ground coriander

garlic

1 Soak 12 wooden skewers in water, to prevent them from burning during broiling. Mix the oil and lemon juice together in a bowl and stir in the cubed chicken. Cover and let marinate for at least 30 minutes.

2 Thread four or five cubes on each wooden skewer. Cook under a hot broiler, turning often, until cooked and browned, about 10 minutes. Cut one piece open to check it is cooked all the way through: this is very important, especially for chicken.

3 Meanwhile make the dip. Mix the chili powder with 1 tbsp water. Heat the oil in a small frying pan and fry the onion and garlic until tender.

4 Turn down the heat and add the chili paste and the remaining ingredients and stir well. Stir in more water if the sauce is too thick and put it into a small bowl. Serve the dip warm, with the chicken kebabs, cucumber slices and lemon wedges.

Super Bowl Soup

Easy to make as there's no need to be too fussy – just chop up lots of your favorite vegetables and simmer them gently with tomatoes and stock. Serve with crusty bread.

Serves 4–6

INGREDIENTS
1 tbsp oil
1 onion, sliced
2 carrots, sliced
1½ lb potatoes, cut in large chunks
5 cups vegetable stock or vegetable cubes in 5 cups water
1 lb can chopped tomatoes
4 oz broccoli, cut in florets
1 zucchini, sliced
1¼ cups mushrooms, sliced
1½ tsp medium-hot curry powder (optional)
1 tsp dried mixed herbs
salt and pepper

1 Heat the oil in a large saucepan and fry the onion and carrots gently, until they start to soften.

vegetable stock

curry powder

onion

zucchini

potatoes

dried mixed herbs

mushrooms

carrots

chopped tomatoes

broccoli florets

2 Add the potatoes and fry gently for 2 minutes more; stir often or they might stick. Add the stock, tomatoes, broccoli, zucchini and mushrooms.

3 Add the curry powder (if using), herbs and salt and pepper and bring to a boil. Put the lid on and simmer gently for 30–40 minutes, or until the vegetables are tender. Taste and add more salt and pepper if needed.

Cock-a-Noodle Soup

Take a tasty trip to the Far East, with this Chinese-style soup.

Serves 4–6

INGREDIENTS
1 tbsp sesame oil
4 scallions, coarsely chopped
8 oz boneless, skinless chicken breasts, cut in small cubes
5 cups chicken stock or cubes and water
1 tbsp soy sauce
1 cup frozen corn niblets
4 oz medium egg-noodles
salt and pepper
1 carrot, thinly sliced lengthwise, to garnish
shrimp crackers, to serve (optional)

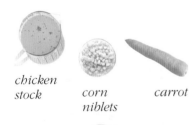

chicken stock

corn niblets

carrot

chicken breast

soy sauce

sesame oil

scallions

medium egg-noodles

1 Heat the oil and fry the scallions and chicken until the meat has browned all over.

2 Add the stock and the soy sauce and bring the soup to a boil.

3 Stir in the corn, then add the noodles, breaking them up roughly. Taste the soup and add salt and pepper if needed.

4 Use small cutters to stamp out shapes from the thin slices of carrot. Add them to the soup. Simmer for 5 minutes, before serving in bowls with shrimp crackers, if you like.

See-in-the-Dark Soup

Stop stumbling around when the lights are off –
eat more carrots! Serve with crunchy toast.

Serves 4

INGREDIENTS
1 tbsp oil
1 onion, sliced
1 lb carrots, sliced
½ cup split red lentils
5 cups vegetable stock
1 tsp ground coriander
3 tbsp chopped fresh parsley
salt and pepper

vegetable stock

onion

parsley

red lentils

carrots

ground coriander

1 Heat the oil and fry the onion until it is starting to brown. Add the sliced carrots and fry gently for 4–5 minutes, stirring them often, until they soften.

3 Add the lentils, stock and coriander to the saucepan with a little salt and pepper. Bring the soup to a boil.

2 Meanwhile, put the lentils in a small bowl and cover with cold water. Pour off any bits that float. Turn the lentils into a strainer and rinse under the cold tap.

4 Turn down the heat, put the lid on and leave to simmer gently for 30 minutes, or until the lentils are cooked.

5 Add the chopped parsley and cook for 5 minutes more. Remove from the heat and allow to cool slightly.

6 Carefully put the soup into a food processor or blender and process until it is smooth. (You may have to do this a half at a time.) Rinse the saucepan before pouring the soup back in and add a little water if it looks too thick. Heat up again before serving.

COOK'S TIP
Push the soup through a strainer with a wooden spoon or leave it chunky, if you don't have a food processor or blender.

Tasty Toasts

Next time friends come over to watch a video, surprise them with these delicious treats.

Serves 4

INGREDIENTS
2 red bell peppers, halved
   lengthwise and seeded
2 tbsp oil
1 garlic clove, peeled and
   crushed
1 French mini-baguette or roll
3 tbsp pesto
⅓ cup French soft goat cheese

1 Put the bell pepper halves, cut-side down, under a hot broiler and let the skins blacken. Carefully put the halves in a paper bag, tie the top and leave them until they are cool enough to handle. Peel off the skins and cut the bell peppers into strips.

garlic

mini-baguette

soft goat cheese

red bell peppers

pesto

oil

2 Put the oil in a small bowl and stir in the garlic. Cut the bread into slanting slices and brush one side with the garlic-flavored oil. Arrange the slices on a broiler pan and brown under a hot broiler.

3 Turn the slices over and brush the untoasted sides with the garlic-flavored oil and then with the pesto.

4 Arrange pepper strips over each slice and put small wedges of goat cheese on top. Put under the broiler and toast until the cheese browns and melts slightly. Serve hot or cold.

Chili Cheese Nachos

Viva Mexico! Silence that hungry tummy with a truly spicy snack. Make it as cool or as hot as you like, by adjusting the amount of sliced jalapeño chilies. Ole!

Serves 4

INGREDIENTS
4 oz bag chili tortilla chips
2 oz Cheddar cheese, grated
2 oz cheese,
  grated
2 oz pickled green jalapeño
  chilies, sliced

FOR THE DIP
2 tbsp lemon or lime juice
1 avocado, coarsely chopped
1 beefsteak tomato, coarsely
  chopped
salt and pepper

I Arrange the tortilla chips in an even layer on a flameproof plate which can be used under the broiler. Sprinkle all the grated cheese over and then sprinkle as many jalapeño chilies as you like over the top.

beefsteak tomato

*pickled green
jalapeño chilies*

*grated Cheddar
cheese*

avocado

lemon juice

*chili tortilla
chips*

*grated
cheese*

2 Put the plate under a hot broiler and toast until the cheese has melted and browned – keep an eye on the chips to make sure they don't burn.

3 Mix the lemon juice, avocado and tomato together in a bowl. Add salt and pepper to taste and serve with the chips.

31

Wicked Tortilla Wedges

This tortilla is a thick omelet with lots of cooked potatoes in it. It is very popular in Spain, where it is cut in thick slices like a cake and served with bread. Try it with sliced tomato salad.

Serves 4

INGREDIENTS
2 tbsp oil
1½ lb potatoes, cut in small
  chunks
1 onion, sliced
1¼ cups mushrooms, sliced
1 cup frozen peas, thawed
⅓ cup frozen corn niblets,
  thawed
4 eggs
⅔ cup milk
2 tsp Cajun seasoning
2 tbsp chopped fresh parsley
salt and pepper

milk *corn*

mushrooms

parsley

eggs *potatoes*

*Cajun
seasoning* *peas*

onion

1 Heat the oil in a large frying pan and fry the potatoes and onion for 3–4 minutes, stirring often. Turn down the heat, cover the pan and fry gently for 8–10 minutes more, until the potatoes are almost tender.

2 Add the mushrooms to the pan and cook for 2–3 minutes more, stirring often, until they have softened.

3 Add the peas and corn and stir them into the potato mixture.

4 Put the eggs, milk and Cajun seasoning in a bowl. Add salt and pepper to taste and beat well.

5 Level the top of the vegetables and sprinkle the parsley on top. Pour the egg mixture over and cook over a low heat for 10–15 minutes.

6 Put the pan under a hot broiler to set the top of the tortilla. Serve hot or cold, cut into wedges.

COOK'S TIP
Use less Cajun seasoning if you don't like spicy food. Make sure the frying pan can be used under the broiler.

Give 'em a Roasting

Don't stick to roast spuds! A good roasting brings out the colors and flavors of other vegetables too.

Serves 4

INGREDIENTS

1 eggplant, cut in large chunks
1 tbsp salt
1 red bell pepper, seeded and cut in thick strips
1 green bell pepper, seeded and cut in thick strips
1 yellow bell pepper, seeded and cut in thick strips
1 zucchini, cut in large chunks
1 onion, cut in thick slices
1¼ cups small mushrooms
8 oz plum tomatoes, quartered
5 tbsp olive oil
4–5 thyme sprigs
2 oregano sprigs
3–4 rosemary sprigs
sea salt and freshly ground black pepper

bell peppers *thyme* *eggplant* *oil* *rosemary* *onion* *zucchini* *plum tomatoes* *mushrooms* *oregano*

1 Arrange the eggplant chunks on a plate and sprinkle them with the salt. Let stand for 30 minutes.

2 Squeeze the eggplant to remove as much liquid as possible. Rinse off the salt. This process stops the eggplant tasting so bitter.

3 Preheat the oven to 400°F. Arrange all the vegetables, including the eggplant, in a roasting pan and drizzle the oil over.

4 Sprinkle most of the herb sprigs in among the vegetables and season well. Put the pan into the hot oven and cook for 20–25 minutes.

5 Turn the vegetables over and cook them for 15 minutes more, or until they are tender and browned.

6 Sprinkle the remaining fresh herb sprigs over the cooked vegetables just before serving.

Chunky Veggy Salad

Something to really sink your teeth into – this salad is chockablock with vitamins and energy. Serve on large slices of crusty bread.

Serves 4

INGREDIENTS
¼ small white cabbage, finely chopped
¼ small red cabbage, finely chopped
8 baby carrots, thinly sliced
⅝ cup small mushrooms, quartered
4 oz cauliflower, cut in small florets
1 small zucchini, grated
4in piece cucumber, cubed
2 tomatoes, coarsely chopped
½ cup sprouted seeds
½ cup salted peanuts
2 tbsp sunflower oil
1 tbsp lemon juice
salt and pepper
2 oz cheese, grated

1 Put all the prepared vegetables and sprouted seeds in a bowl together and mix well.

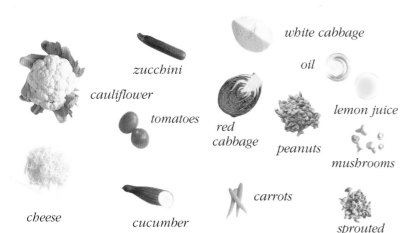

zucchini

white cabbage

oil

cauliflower

tomatoes

red cabbage

lemon juice

peanuts

mushrooms

cheese

cucumber

carrots

sprouted seeds

2 Stir in the peanuts. Drizzle the oil and lemon juice over. Season well and let stand for 30 minutes to allow the flavor to develop.

3 Sprinkle grated cheese over just before serving on large slices of crusty bread. Have extra dressing ready, in case anybody wants more.

Yellow Chicken

An all-time Chinese favorite that you can stir-fry in a few minutes. Serve with boiled rice.

Serves 4

INGREDIENTS
2 tbsp oil
¾ cup salted cashews
4 scallions, coarsely chopped
1 lb boneless, skinless
   chicken breasts, cut in strips
5 oz jar Chinese bean sauce

1 Heat 1 tbsp of the oil in a frying pan and fry the cashews until browned. This does not take long, so keep an eye on them. Lift them out with a slotted spoon and put them to one side.

Chinese bean sauce

scallions

chicken

2 Heat the remaining oil and fry the scallions and chicken for 5–8 minutes, until the meat is browned all over and cooked.

cashews

oil

3 Return the nuts to the pan and pour the jar of sauce over. Stir well and cook gently until hot. Serve at once.

COOK'S TIP

Cashews are quite expensive, but you can buy broken cashews, which are cheaper and perfectly good for this dish. You could also use almonds, if you prefer.

Pepperoni Pasta

Add extra zip to bland and boring pasta dishes with spicy pepperoni sausage.

Serves 4

INGREDIENTS
2½ cups dried pasta
6 oz pepperoni sausage, sliced
1 small or ½ large red onion, sliced
3 tbsp green pesto
⅔ cup heavy cream
8 oz cherry tomatoes, halved
½ oz fresh chives
salt

cherry tomatoes

green pesto

pasta

heavy cream

fresh chives

red onion

pepperoni sausage

1 Cook the pasta in a large pan of lightly salted, boiling water, following the instructions on the package.

2 Meanwhile, gently fry the pepperoni sausage slices and the onion together in a frying pan until the onion is soft. The oil from the sausage will mean you won't need extra oil.

3 Mix the pesto sauce and cream together in a small bowl.

4 Add this mixture to the frying pan and stir until the sauce is smooth.

5 Add the cherry tomatoes and snip the chives over the top with scissors. Stir again.

6 Drain the pasta and tip it back into the pan. Pour the sauce over and mix well, making sure all the pasta is coated. Serve immediately.

COOK'S TIP
Use a mixture of red and yellow cherry tomatoes for a really colorful meal. Serve with sesame bread sticks.

Pancake Packages

Be adventurous with your pancakes! Don't just stick to lemon and sugar: try this tasty version for a real change.

Serves 4

INGREDIENTS
FOR THE PANCAKES
1 cup all-purpose flour
1 egg
1¼ cups milk
½ tsp salt
2 tbsp butter, for frying

FOR THE FILLING
scant 1 cup cream cheese with chives
6 tbsp heavy cream
4 oz ham, cut in strips
4 oz cheese, grated
¼ cup fresh breadcrumbs
salt and pepper

breadcrumbs
butter
cream
flour
cheese
milk
ham
cream cheese with chives
egg

1 To make the pancakes, put the flour, egg, a little milk and the salt in a bowl and beat together with a wooden spoon. Gradually beat in the rest of the milk until the batter looks like heavy cream. (The milk must be added slowly or the batter will be lumpy.)

2 Melt a little butter in a medium-size frying pan and pour in just enough batter to cover the base in a thin layer. Tilt and turn the pan to spread the batter out. Cook gently until set, then turn over with a metal spatula and cook the second side. If you feel brave enough try tossing the pancakes!

3 Slide the pancake out of the pan. Stack them in a pile, with a piece of wax paper between each one to keep them from sticking to each other. There should be enough batter to make four large pancakes. Preheat the oven to 375°F.

4 Make the filling. Beat the cream cheese and cream in a bowl. Add the ham and half the cheese; season well. Put a spoonful of the mixture in the center of a pancake.

5 Fold one side over the mixture and then the other. Fold both ends up as well to make a small package. Arrange the packages on a baking sheet, with the joins underneath. Make three more packages in the same way.

6 Sprinkle the remaining cheese and the breadcrumbs over the packages and cover with foil. Cook for 20 minutes. Remove the foil. Cook for 10 minutes more, until browned. Tie green scallions around the parcels, if you like.

Eggs in a Blanket

A hearty brunch or lunch to tuck into on a chilly day, with chunks of wholewheat bread.

Serves 4

INGREDIENTS
1 eggplant, sliced
1 tsp salt
1 tbsp oil
1 onion, sliced
1 garlic clove, peeled and
  crushed
1 yellow bell pepper, seeded
  and sliced
1 zucchini, sliced
15 oz can chopped tomatoes
½ cup water
2 tsp dried mixed herbs
4 eggs
salt and pepper

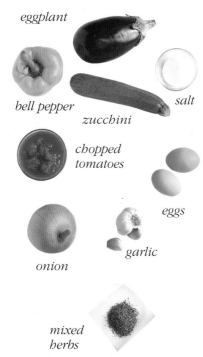

eggplant

bell pepper

zucchini

salt

chopped tomatoes

eggs

garlic

onion

mixed herbs

1 Arrange the eggplant slices on a plate, sprinkle with salt and let stand for 30 minutes. Rinse and squeeze out as much juice as you can.

2 Heat the oil in a large frying pan. Fry the onion until it begins to soften. Add the garlic, bell pepper, zucchini and eggplant and fry for 3–4 minutes.

3 Add the chopped tomatoes, water and herbs. Stir in salt and pepper to taste. Simmer gently for 5 minutes.

4 Make four shallow depressions in the mixture and break an egg into each one. Cover the pan with a lid and simmer for 8–12 minutes, until the eggs are set and the vegetables are tender.

Chicken Chips

Forget all that spud-bashing – top your pie with a package of chips instead.

Serves 4

INGREDIENTS
1 cup dried pasta shapes
6 oz broccoli, cut in florets
4 tbsp butter
1 red onion, thinly sliced
8 strips lean bacon, chopped
8 oz boneless, skinless chicken
  breasts, cut in chunks
¼ cup all-purpose flour
scant 2 cups milk
salt and pepper

FOR THE TOPPING
3 small packages of chips
3 oz cheese, grated

butter

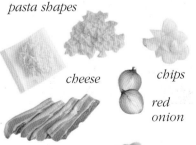
milk *flour* *broccoli*

pasta shapes

cheese *chips*

red onion

bacon

chicken

1 Cook the pasta in lightly salted, boiling water for 5 minutes. Add the broccoli and cook for 5 minutes more, until the pasta and broccoli are tender. Drain well.

2 Meanwhile, melt the butter in a saucepan and fry the onion until it begins to soften. Add the bacon and chicken and fry gently until browned all over. Add the flour and mix well.

3 Take the pan off the heat and very gradually mix in the milk. Season, return to the heat and bring to a boil, stirring all the time. Stir in the drained pasta and broccoli. Tip the mixture into a dish that can go under a broiler.

4 Preheat the broiler. Cover the top of the mixture with the chips and sprinkle with the cheese. Put under the hot broiler for a few minutes, until the cheese has melted and browned.

Something Very Fishy

If you like getting down and dirty, this is the recipe for you! Serve with green vegetables and new potatoes.

Serves 4

INGREDIENTS
1 lb old potatoes, cut in
  small chunks
2 tbsp butter or margarine
1 tbsp milk
15 oz can pink salmon, drained,
  with skin and bones removed
1 egg, beaten
¼ cup all-purpose flour
2 scallions, finely chopped
4 sun-dried tomatoes in oil,
  chopped
grated rind of 1 lemon
¼ cup sesame seeds
oil, for shallow-frying
salt and pepper

salmon

butter

milk

potatoes

egg

flour

scallions

lemon

sesame seeds

sun-dried
tomatoes

1 Cook the potatoes in boiling lightly salted water until tender. Drain and return to the saucepan. Add the butter or margarine and milk and mash until smooth. Season well.

2 Put the mashed potato in a bowl and beat in the salmon. Add the egg, flour, scallions, tomatoes and lemon rind. Mix well.

3 Divide the mixture into eight equal pieces and pat them into fish cake shapes, using floured hands.

4 Put the sesame seeds on a large plate and very gently press both sides of the fish cakes into them, until the cakes are lightly coated.

5 Pour oil into a frying pan to a depth of about ⅛in. Heat it gently. Put a small cube of bread in the pan and, if it sizzles, the oil is ready to cook the fish cakes. You will need to cook the fish cakes in several batches.

6 When one side is crisp and brown turn the cakes over carefully with a spatula and a fork, to cook the second side. The fish cakes are quite soft and need gentle treatment or they will break up. Lift them out and put them to drain on kitchen towels. Keep hot until they are all cooked.

COOK'S TIP
Use canned tuna instead of the salmon, if you prefer.

Sticky Fingers

You have to like messy food to eat this popular dish, so plenty of napkins please! Juicy tomatoes make a refreshing accompaniment.

Serves 4

INGREDIENTS
2 tbsp oil
1 onion, chopped
1 garlic clove, crushed
2 tbsp tomato paste
1 tbsp white wine vinegar
3 tbsp clear honey
1 tsp dried mixed herbs
½ tsp chili powder
⅔ cup chicken stock
8 chicken thighs
¾ lb spare ribs

FOR THE POTATOES
1½ lb potatoes, cubed
2 tbsp oil
1 large onion, sliced
1 garlic clove, crushed
salt and pepper

chicken stock

onion

spare ribs

tomato paste

chili powder

vinegar

potatoes

honey

garlic

chicken thighs

mixed herbs

1 Heat the oil in a saucepan and fry the onion and garlic until the onion begins to soften.

2 Add the tomato paste, vinegar, honey, herbs, chili powder and stock and bring to a boil. Lower the heat and simmer for 15–20 minutes, when the sauce should have thickened.

3 Preheat the oven to 375°F. Arrange the chicken and ribs in a roasting pan.

4 Spoon the sauce evenly over the meat and cook for 30 minutes. Turn the meat over to ensure that it is coated evenly in the sauce.

5 Cook for 45 minutes more, turning the meat several times and spooning the sauce over. The meat should be really browned and sticky.

6 Meanwhile, put the potatoes in lightly salted water, bring to a boil, then drain well. Heat the oil in a large frying pan. Fry the onion until it begins to turn brown. Add the potatoes and garlic and fry for 25–30 minutes, until everything is cooked through, browned and crisp.

Tiny Toads

Serve these pint-sized portions of toad-in-the-hole with peas.

Serves 4

INGREDIENTS
1 cup all-purpose flour
1 egg
1¼ cups milk
3 tbsp fresh mixed herbs,
   e.g. parsley, thyme and chives,
   coarsely chopped
24 cocktail sausages
salt and pepper

FOR THE ONION GRAVY
1 tbsp oil
2 onions, sliced
2½ cups stock
1 tbsp soy sauce
1 tbsp whole-grain mustard
2 tbsp cornstarch
2 tbsp water

stock
milk
onions
mustard
sausages
soy sauce
flour *cornstarch* *chives*
thyme
egg *parsley*

1 Preheat the oven to 400°F. Put the flour, egg and a little milk in a bowl and mix well with a wooden spoon. Gradually mix in the rest of the milk to make a batter. Season well with salt and pepper and stir in the herbs.

2 Lightly oil eight 4in nonstick baking pans and arrange three sausages in each. Place in the hot oven and cook for 10 minutes.

COOK'S TIP

Use vegetarian sausages for friends who don't eat meat.

3 Carefully take the pans out of the oven and use a ladle to pour batter into each pan. Put them back in the oven and cook for 30–40 minutes more, until the batter is risen and browned.

4 Meanwhile, heat the oil in a pan. Fry the onions for 15 minutes until really browned. Add the stock, soy and mustard and bring to a boil. Mix the cornstarch and water together in a cup and pour into the gravy. Bring to a boil, stirring. Serve with the "toads."

Cherry Tomato Pizza

This looks sort of like a pizza but tastes very different.

Serves 4

INGREDIENTS
2 cups all-purpose flour
1 tsp salt
1 envelope rapid-rise yeast
⅞ cup hand-hot water
1 egg, beaten
3 tbsp poppy seeds
2 red bell peppers, seeded and
  cut in strips
1 red onion, cut in strips
½ lb cherry tomatoes, halved
3 tbsp olive oil
salt and black pepper
fresh basil leaves, to garnish

flour

water

*bell
peppers*

basil

egg

tomatoes

*poppy
seeds*

red onion

yeast

olive oil

1 Put the flour, salt and yeast in a bowl and mix well. Add half the water and mix with a knife. Add the rest of the water and use your hands to pull the mixture together to make a dough.

2 Put the dough on a lightly floured surface and knead for 5 minutes, until it is no longer sticky but smooth and stretchy. Put in a bowl, cover with plastic wrap and leave for 30–45 minutes in a warm place, such as an airing cupboard, until doubled in size.

3 Meanwhile, preheat the oven to 400°F. Knead the dough again and roll or press it out into a rectangular shape about ¼in thick. Put it on a baking sheet and brush the edges with the beaten egg. Sprinkle the edges with poppy seeds. Sprinkle the prepared vegetables on the unseeded central area and drizzle the oil over the top. Sprinkle with salt and pepper and cook for 30–40 minutes, until the dough has risen and browned and the vegetables have cooked. Garnish with basil and serve hot or cold.

Raving Ravioli

Have a rockin' good time making your own
pasta – get your friends to help.

Serves 4

INGREDIENTS
3oz fresh spinach, torn up, with
  tough stalks removed
2½ cups all-purpose flour
3 eggs, beaten
1 tbsp oil
1¼ cups heavy cream
1 tbsp chopped fresh cilantro
2 tbsp grated Parmesan cheese,
  plus extra to serve
salt and pepper

FOR THE FILLING
4 oz trout fillet, poached and
  drained, skin and bones
  removed
⅓ cup ricotta cheese
grated rind of 1 lemon
1 tbsp chopped fresh cilantro
salt and pepper

eggs
cream
spinach
oil
trout fillet
flour
lemon
Parmesan cheese
ricotta cheese
fresh cilantro

1 Steam the spinach over a pan of boiling water until it wilts. Let cool, and squeeze out as much water as possible Put into a food processor, along with the flour, eggs, oil and salt and pepper and process until the mixture forms a dough.

2 Place the dough on a lightly floured surface and knead it for 5 minutes, until smooth. Wrap it in plastic wrap and chill in the fridge for 30 minutes.

3 Sprinkle the work surface with flour. Roll the dough out to make a 20 × 18in shape, so the dough is the thickness of card. Let dry for 15 minutes. Use a sharp knife or pastry wheel to trim the edges and cut the dough in half.

4 Put the trout in a small bowl. Add the ricotta cheese, lemon rind, the cilantro and salt and pepper and beat together. Put four spoonfuls of the filling across the top of the dough, leaving a small border around the edge. Continue putting the filling mixture in lines, to make eight rows. Lift up the second sheet of pasta on a rolling pin and lay it gently over the first sheet.

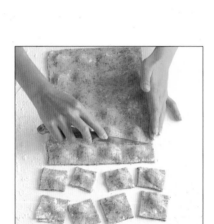

5 Run your finger between the bumps to remove any air and press the dough together. Using a knife or pastry wheel, cut the ravioli into small packages and trim around the edge as well, to seal each one. Cook in lightly salted boiling water for 8–10 minutes. Drain and return to the pan.

6 Put the cream, remaining cilantro and the Parmesan in a small saucepan and heat gently, without boiling. Pour over the ravioli and stir until evenly coated. Serve immediately, with more Parmesan handed round, if you like.

Homeburgers

These look the same as ordinary burgers, but watch out for the soft, cheese center. Serve with French fries and sliced tomatoes.

Serves 4

INGREDIENTS
1 lb lean ground beef
2 slices of bread, crusts removed
1 egg
4 scallions, coarsely chopped
1 garlic clove, peeled and chopped
1 tbsp mango chutney
2 tsp dried mixed herbs
⅓ cup mozzarella cheese
salt and pepper
4 hamburger buns, to serve

ground beef

bread

scallions

mozzarella cheese

egg

garlic

mango chutney

mixed herbs

1 Put the ground beef, bread, egg, scallions and garlic in a food processor. Add a little salt and pepper and process until evenly blended. Add the chutney and herbs and process again.

2 Divide the mixture into four equal portions and pat flat, with damp hands, to keep the meat from sticking.

3 Cut the cheese into four equal pieces and put one in the center of each piece of beef. Wrap the meat around the cheese to make a fat hamburger. Chill for 30 minutes. Preheat the broiler.

4 Put the burgers on a rack under the hot broiler, but not too close or they will burn on the outside before the middle has cooked properly. Cook them for 5–8 minutes on each side then put each burger in a bun with your favorite trimmings.

Popeye's Pie

Tuck into this layered pie and you, too, can have bulging muscles!

Serves 4

INGREDIENTS
6 tbsp butter
1 tsp grated nutmeg
2 lb fresh spinach, washed and
   large stalks removed
⅔ cup feta cheese, crumbled
2 oz Cheddar cheese, grated
10 oz filo pastry sheets
2 tsp mixed ground cinnamon,
   nutmeg and black pepper

1 Melt 2 tbsp of the butter in a large frying pan, add the nutmeg and the spinach and season well. Cover and cook for 5 minutes, or until the spinach is tender. Drain well, pressing out as much liquid as possible.

spinach   *filo pastry*

feta cheese   *black pepper*

nutmeg   *cinnamon*

butter   *Cheddar cheese*

2 Preheat the oven to 325°F. Melt the remaining butter in a small saucepan. Mix the cheeses together in a bowl and season them with salt and pepper. Unfold the pastry so the sheets are flat. Use one to line part of the bottom of a small, deep-sided, greased roasting pan. Brush with melted butter. Keep the remaining filo sheets covered with a damp dish towel: they dry out very quickly.

3 Continue to lay pastry sheets across the bottom and up the sides of the pan, brushing each time with butter, until two-thirds of the pastry has been used. Don't worry if they flop over the top edges – they will be tidied up later.

4 Mix together the grated cheeses and spinach and spread them into the pan. Fold the pastry edges over. Crumple up the remaining sheets of pastry and arrange them over the top of the filling. Brush with melted butter and sprinkle the mixed spices over the top. Cook the pie for 45 minutes. Raise the oven temperature to 400°F, for 10–15 minutes more, to brown the top. Serve hot or cold.

Turkey Surprise Packages

This looks just like a paper package but there's a special treat inside. Put a package on each plate, with new potatoes and green vegetables, and let everyone open their own surprise.

COOK'S TIP
Fennel tastes like aniseed or liquorice, so leave it out if you don't like that flavor.

Serves 4

INGREDIENTS
2 tbsp chopped parsley
4 turkey breast cutlets, weighing
  5–6 oz each
8 strips lean bacon
2 scallions, cut in thin strips
2 oz fennel bulb, cut in thin
  strips
1 carrot, cut in thin strips
1 small celery stalk, cut in thin
  strips
grated rind and juice of 1 lemon
salt and pepper
lemon wedges, to serve

lemon
celery
scallions
fennel bulb
turkey
bacon
parsley

1 Pat parsley over each turkey breast cutlet, then wrap two strips of bacon around each one.

2 Preheat the oven to 375°F. Cut four 12in circles out of wax paper and put a turkey breast just off center on each one.

3 Arrange the vegetable strips on top of the cutlets, sprinkle the lemon rind and juice over and season well with salt and pepper.

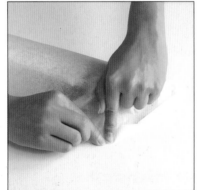

4 Fold the paper over the meat and vegetables and, starting at one side, twist and fold the paper edges together.

5 Work your way around the semi-circle, to seal the edges of the package together neatly.

6 Put all four packages in a roasting pan and cook for 35–45 minutes, or until the meat is cooked and tender. Make sure that the cutlets are cooked all the way through. Serve the packages with the lemon wedges to squeeze over them.

Fish 'n' Rice

This tasty paella-type meal uses a frozen fish mixture that saves lots of preparation time.

Serves 4

INGREDIENTS
2 tbsp oil
1 onion, sliced
1 red bell pepper, seeded and chopped
1¼ cups mushrooms, chopped
2 tsp ground turmeric
6–7 oz package quick cooking mixed grains or pilaf rice and grains
3 cups stock, made with seasonings in package
14 oz frozen premium seafood selection, thawed
4 oz frozen jumbo shrimp, thawed
salt and pepper

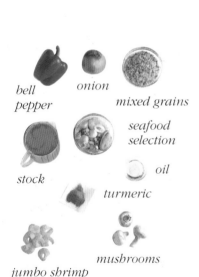

bell pepper *onion* *mixed grains*

seafood selection

stock *oil*

turmeric

jumbo shrimp *mushrooms*

1 Heat the oil in a deep frying pan and fry the onion until it is beginning to soften. Add the chopped bell pepper and mushrooms and fry for 1 minute.

2 Stir in the turmeric and then the grains. Stir until well mixed, then carefully pour on the stock. Season with salt and pepper, cover with a lid and let simmer gently for 15 minutes.

3 Add the seafood selection and the shrimp, stir well and turn up the heat slightly to bring the liquid back to a boil. Cover again and simmer for 15–20 minutes more, until the grains are cooked and the fish is hot. Serve the fish immediately.

COOK'S TIP

Choose your fish mixture from the frozen food lockers in your market. If using only shrimp, scallops and crab, cut down on the cooking time.

Honey Chops

These tasty sticky chops are very quick and easy to prepare and broil, but they would be just as good barbecued. Serve with herby mashed potatoes or French fries.

Serves 4

INGREDIENTS
1 lb carrots
1 tbsp butter
1 tbsp brown sugar
1 tbsp sesame seeds

FOR THE CHOPS
4 pork loin chops
4 tbsp butter
2 tbsp clear honey
1 tbsp tomato paste

carrots

honey

butter

tomato paste

pork loin chops

sesame seeds

brown sugar

1 Cut the carrots into matchstick shapes, put them in a saucepan and just cover them with cold water. Add the butter and brown sugar and bring to a boil. Turn down the heat and let simmer for 15–20 minutes, until most of the liquid has boiled away.

2 Line the broiler pan with foil and arrange the pork chops on the broiler rack. Beat the butter and honey together and gradually beat in the tomato paste, to make a smooth paste. Preheat the broiler to high.

3 Spread half the honey paste over the chops and broil them for 5 minutes, until browned.

4 Carefully turn the chops over, spread them with the remaining honey paste and return to the broiler. Broil the second side for 5 minutes more, or until the meat is cooked through. Sprinkle the sesame seeds over the carrots and serve with the chops.

COOK'S TIP

If the chops are very thick, put them under a medium-hot broiler for longer to make sure they are cooked in the middle.

Party Lamb

Racks of lamb are actually lamb chops, called a "crown roast", that are still joined together.

Serves 4

INGREDIENTS
2 racks of lamb, with at least
    four chops in each piece
2 tbsp butter
4 scallions, coarsely chopped
⅜ cup basmati rice
1¼ cups stock
1 large ripe mango, peeled and
    coarsely chopped
salt and pepper

FOR THE ROAST POTATOES
2 lb potatoes, peeled and cut in
    large, even pieces
2 tbsp oil
1 tbsp coarse sea or kosher salt

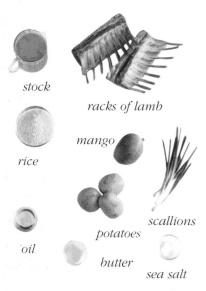

stock

racks of lamb

mango

rice

potatoes

scallions

oil

butter

sea salt

COOK'S TIP
Ask your butcher to prepare the meat for you when you buy it. Serve with minty peas.

1 Use a sharp knife to cut the meat off the ends of the bones. Discard the thick, fatty skin and scrape the bones as clean as possible. Chop the trimmings into small pieces and save them for the stuffing. (The butcher can do all this, if you prefer.)

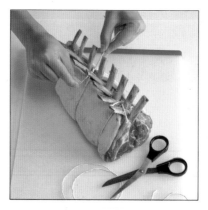

2 Interlock the bones like fingers and tie the two sides together with a piece of string between each two chops. Stand them in a roasting pan.

3 Melt the butter in a saucepan, add the scallions and lamb trimmings and fry until the meat has browned. Add the rice, stir well and pour in the stock. Bring to a boil, lower the heat, put a lid on the pan and let simmer for 8–10 minutes, until the rice is tender.

4 Remove from the heat, stir in the mango and taste the stuffing. Add salt and pepper. Preheat the oven to 375°F.

5 Put the stuffing in the middle of the chops. Wrap the ends of the bones in a thin strip of foil and put the pan in the oven. Cook for 30 minutes.

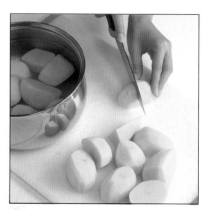

6 Meanwhile, make deep cuts in the rounded side of each potato and put them in a saucepan with cold, salted water. Bring to a boil. Drain and arrange around the outside of the meat. Drizzle the oil over, sprinkle with sea salt and put back in the oven for 1–1½ hours more, until the potatoes are crisp and the meat is cooked.

DAZZLING DESSERTS

Chocolate Cream Puffs

These are always a big favorite and so easy and cheap to make.

Serves 4–6

INGREDIENTS
⅔ cup water
4 tbsp butter
⅝ cup all-purpose flour, sifted
2 eggs, beaten

FOR THE FILLING AND ICING
⅔ cup heavy cream
1½ cups confectioner's sugar
1 tbsp cocoa
2–4 tbsp water

flour

water

cream

confectioner's sugar

cocoa

butter

eggs

COOK'S TIP
If the unfilled profiteroles get soggy, put them back into a hot oven for a few minutes and they will crisp up again.

1 Put the water in a saucepan, add the butter and heat gently until it melts. Bring to a boil and remove from the heat. Put in all the flour at once and beat quickly until the mixture sticks together, leaving the side of the pan clean. Let cool slightly.

2 Add the eggs, a little at a time, to the mixture and beat well each time, by hand with a wooden spoon or with electric beaters until the mixture is thick and glossy and drops reluctantly from a spoon (you may not need to use all of the egg). Preheat the oven to 425°F.

3 Dampen two baking sheets with cold water and put walnut-size spoonfuls of the mixture on them. Leave some space for them to rise. Cook for 25–30 minutes, until they are golden brown and well risen. Use a metal spatula to lift them on to a wire rack and make a small hole in each one with the handle of a wooden spoon to allow the steam to escape. Let cool.

4 Make the filling and icing. Whip the cream until thick. Put it into a pastry bag fitted with a plain or star nozzle. Push the nozzle into the hole in each puff and squirt a little cream inside. Put the confectioner's sugar and cocoa in a small bowl and stir together. Add enough water to make a thick glossy icing. Spread a spoonful of icing on each puff and serve.

Let's Get Tropical

Supermarkets are full of weird and wonderful fruits that make a really tangy salad when mixed together. Serve with cream or yogurt.

Serves 4

INGREDIENTS
1 small pineapple
2 kiwi fruit
1 ripe mango
1 watermelon slice
2 peaches
2 bananas
4 tbsp tropical fruit juice

tropical fruit juice

watermelon

mango

pineapple

peaches   *kiwi fruit*   *bananas*

1 Cut the pineapple into ½in slices. Work around the edge of each slice, cutting off the skin and any spiky bits. Cut each slice into wedges and put them in a bowl.

2 Use a potato peeler to remove the skin from the kiwi fruit. Cut them in half lengthwise and then into wedges. Add to the fruit bowl.

3 Cut the mango lengthwise into quarters and cut round the large flat pit. Peel the mango flesh and cut it into chunks or slices.

4 Cut the watermelon into slices, cut off the skin and cut the flesh into chunks. Remove the seeds. Cut the peaches in half, remove the pits and cut the flesh into wedges. Slice the bananas. Add all the fruit to the bowl and gently stir in the fruit juice.

Monster Meringues

A mouthwatering dessert made from meringue, whipped cream and tangy summer fruits.

Serves 4

INGREDIENTS
3 egg whites
¾ cup sugar
1 tbsp cornstarch
1 tsp white wine vinegar
few drops vanilla extract
8 oz assorted red summer fruits
1¼ cups heavy cream
1 passionfruit, if available

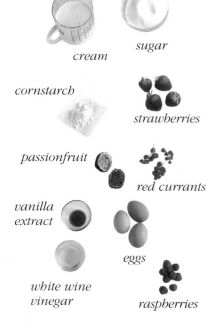

cream

sugar

cornstarch

strawberries

passionfruit

red currants

vanilla extract

eggs

white wine vinegar

raspberries

1 Preheat the oven to 275°F. In pencil, draw eight 4in circles on two separate sheets of wax paper which will fit on two flat baking sheets.

2 Put the egg whites into a very clean, dry bowl and beat until stiff. This will take about 2 minutes with an electric beater; peaks made in the meringue should keep their shape when it's ready. Add the sugar gradually and beat well each time. The mixture should now be very stiff.

3 Use a metal spoon to gently stir in the cornstarch, white wine vinegar and vanilla extract. Put the meringue into a large pastry bag, fitted with a large star nozzle.

COOK'S TIP

Draw six 3in circles and pipe smaller meringues, if you aren't hungry enough for a monster dessert.

4 Pipe a solid layer of meringue in four of the drawn circles and then pipe a lattice pattern in the other four. Put the meringues in the oven and cook for 1¼–1½ hours, swapping shelf positions after 30 minutes, until lightly browned. The paper will peel off the back easily when the meringues are cooked.

5 Coarsely chop most of the summer fruits, reserving a few for decoration. Whip the cream and spread it over the solid meringue shapes. Sprinkle the fruit over. Halve the passionfruit, scoop out the seeds with a teaspoon and sprinkle them over the fruit. Put a lattice lid on top of each and serve with the reserved fruits.

Lazy Apple Turnover

You don't need to be neat to make this dessert as it looks best when it's really craggy and rough. Serve with whipped cream or custard.

Serves 6

INGREDIENTS
2 cups all-purpose flour
1 tbsp sugar
1 tbsp ground cinnamon,
⅔ cup butter or margarine
1 egg, separated
1 lb cooking apples
2 tbsp lemon juice
⅔ cup raisins
½ cup demerara or raw sugar
¼ cup hazelnuts, toasted and
   chopped

lemon   flour   apples

egg

butter   demerara   hazelnuts
          sugar

sugar

raisins

cinnamon

COOK'S TIP
This dessert is delicious served either hot or cold.

1 Put the flour, sugar and spice in a bowl and stir. Add the butter or margarine and work it into the flour with your fingertips, until the mixture looks like breadcrumbs. Add the egg yolk and use your hands to pull the mixture together to make the pastry. (You may need to add a little water.)

2 Turn onto a lightly floured surface and knead gently until smooth. Roll out the pastry to make a rough circle about 12in across. Use the rolling pin to lift the pastry on to a small baking sheet. The pastry should hang over the edges.

3 Peel and slice the apples. Toss them in the lemon juice, to keep them from turning brown. Sprinkle some of them over the middle of the pastry, leaving a 4in border all around. Reserve 2 tbsp of the demerara or raw sugar. Sprinkle some of the raisins over the top, then some of the remaining demerara or raw sugar. Keep making layers of apple, raisins and sugar until you have used them up.

4 Preheat the oven to 400°F. Fold up the pastry edges to cover the fruit, overlapping it where necessary. Don't worry too much about neatness. Brush the pastry with the egg white and sprinkle over the reserved demerara or raw sugar. Sprinkle the nuts over. Cover the central hole with foil, to stop the raisins from burning. Cook for 30–35 minutes, until the pastry is cooked and browned.

Broiled Peaches

A simple, rich dessert that's quick and easy to make. Serve it solo or with cream or yogurt.

Serves 4

INGREDIENTS
1 cup raspberries
2 tbsp confectioner's sugar
4 ripe peaches
8 tbsp mascarpone cheese
3 tbsp brown sugar

peaches

*confectioner's
sugar*

*brown
sugar*

raspberries

*mascarpone
cheese*

COOK'S TIP
As the cheese melts, the sugar might slip off, so have some extra handy to sprinkle over the top of the peaches.

1 Reserve a few of the raspberries for decoration and put the rest in a blender with the confectioner's sugar. Blend until smooth. Use a hand-held blender if you prefer, or push the raspberries through a strainer with a wooden spoon and then mix with the sugar.

2 Cut around each peach lengthwise and twist the fruit. One half should come away, leaving the pit in the second half. Scoop the pit out and arrange all eight halves on a broiler pan, cut-sides up. Preheat the broiler.

3 Put 1 tbsp of cheese in the center of each peach, in the dip left by the pit. Sprinkle the sugar over the top of all the peaches and broil under a medium heat, until the cheese and sugar have just melted.

4 Divide the raspberry sauce among four plates and arrange the broiled peaches on top. Decorate with the reserved fruit and serve immediately.

Summer Fruit Cheesecake

Making this is much easier than it looks and it tastes so good, it's well worth the effort.

Serves 8–10

INGREDIENTS
¾ cup butter
8 oz whole wheat cookies
rind and juice of 2 lemons
1 envelope gelatin
1 cup plain cottage cheese
scant 1 cup soft cream cheese
15 oz can condensed milk
4 cups strawberries
1 cup raspberries

condensed
milk

butter

lemons

cottage
cheese

raspberries

cream
cheese

whole wheat
cookies

strawberries

gelatin

COOK'S TIP
Always add gelatin to the liquid, never the other way round.

1 Cut a piece of wax paper to fit the base of an 8 in springform cake pan with removable rim. Melt the butter in a saucepan over a low heat. Break the cookies in pieces, put them in a food processor and process until they are crumbs. Stir them into the melted butter until well mixed.

2 Tip the crumbs into the cake pan and use a spoon to spread the mixture in a thin, even layer over the bottom, pressing down well. Put the pan in the fridge while you make the filling.

3 Put the lemon rind and juice in a small bowl and sprinkle the gelatin over. Stand the bowl in a saucepan of water and heat gently, until the gelatin crystals have all melted. Stir the mixture and let cool slightly.

4 Put the cottage cheese in a food processor and process for 20 seconds. Add the cream cheese and condensed milk, fix the lid in place again and process the mixture. Pour in the dissolved gelatin mixture and process once more.

5 Coarsely chop half the strawberries and sprinkle them over the cookie base. Add half the raspberries, saving the rest for decorating the top. Pour the cheese mixture carefully over the fruit and smooth the top. Return to the fridge and let set overnight.

6 Carefully loosen the edges of the cheesecake with a metal spatula. Then stand the cake pan on a large mug or can and gently open the clip at the side of the pan. Allow the pan to slide down. Put the cheesecake on a large serving plate and decorate it with the reserved fruit.

Chocolate Cups

Perfect for the chocoholics in the family. Serve with crisp cookies.

Serves 4

INGREDIENTS
7 oz bar semisweet chocolate
½ cup heavy cream
3 oz white chocolate

heavy cream

white chocolate

semisweet chocolate

1 Break half the semisweet chocolate into pieces and put them in a bowl. Stand the bowl over a pan of hot, but not boiling, water and let melt, stirring occasionally. Make sure the water doesn't touch the bowl.

2 Line four ramekins, or similarly sized cups, with a piece of foil. Don't worry about it creasing or scrunching up.

3 Use a clean paintbrush to brush the melted chocolate over the foil in a thick layer. Chill in the fridge until set. Paint a second layer and let chill again.

4 Put the cream in a bowl and whisk until stiff. Melt the remaining semisweet chocolate as before and use a metal spoon to fold it into the cream.

5 Coarsely chop the white chocolate and stir it gently into the chocolate and cream mixture.

6 Carefully peel the foil off the chocolate cups and fill each one with the chocolate and cream mixture. Chill until set.

COOK'S TIP
Try using white chocolate chips , chocolate-covered raisins or a chopped chocolate bar, instead of the white chocolate.

Ice Cream Bombes

This frozen dessert with warm sauce will have you ready to explode – it's dynamite!

Serves 6

INGREDIENTS
4 cups chocolate ice cream
2 cups vanilla ice cream
⅓ cup semisweet chocolate
  chips
4 oz butterscotch chips
5 tbsp heavy cream

*heavy
cream*

*vanilla
ice cream*

*chocolate
chips*

*chocolate
ice cream*

*butterscotch
chips*

1 Divide the chocolate ice cream between six small cups. Push it roughly to the bottom and up the sides, leaving a small cup-shaped depression in the middle. Don't worry if it's not very neat; it will be frozen anyway. Return to the freezer and leave for 45 minutes. Take it out again and smooth the ice cream into shape. Return to the freezer.

2 Put the vanilla ice cream in a small bowl and break it up slightly with a spoon. Stir in the chocolate chips and then use this mixture to fill the depression in the chocolate ice cream. Return the cups to the freezer and leave overnight.

3 Put the butterscotch chips in a small saucepan and heat gently, stirring all the time. As they melt, add the heavy cream and keep mixing until all the butterscotch chips have melted and the sauce is warm.

4 Dip the cups in hot water and run a knife around the edge of the ice cream. Turn out onto individual plates and pour the butterscotch sauce over the top. Serve immediately.

Puffy Pears

An eye-catching dessert that is simple to make and delicious to eat, especially when served with whipped cream or mascarpone.

Serves 4

INGREDIENTS
8 oz puff pastry
2 pears, peeled
2 squares semisweet chocolate, coarsely chopped
1 tbsp lemon juice
1 egg, beaten
1 tbsp sugar

puff pastry

pears

egg

sugar

lemon juice

semisweet chocolate

1 Roll the pastry into a 10in square on a lightly floured surface. Trim the edges, then cut it into four equal smaller squares.

2 Remove the core from each pear half and pack the gap with the chopped chocolate. Place a pear half, cut-side down, on each piece of pastry and brush them with the lemon juice, to keep them from going brown.

3 Preheat the oven to 375°F. Cut the pastry into a pear shape, by following the lines of the fruit, leaving a 1in border. Use the trimmings to make leaves and brush the pastry border with the beaten egg.

4 Arrange the pastry and pears on a baking sheet. Make deep cuts in the pears, taking care not to cut all the way through the fruit, and sprinkle them with the sugar. Cook for 20–25 minutes, until lightly browned. Serve hot or cold.

COOK'S TIP
Try the same thing using eating apples, especially when you have picked the fruit yourself.

Chocolate Brownies

Scout out these delicious, moist and chewy cakes, and guide yourself to a chocolate treat!

Makes 9

INGREDIENTS
4½ tbsp butter
2 oz semisweet chocolate
scant 1 cup brown sugar
2 eggs, beaten
⅝ cup all-purpose flour
½ cup coarsely chopped pecans
  or walnuts
¼ cup confectioner's sugar

confectioner's sugar

brown sugar

flour

butter

eggs

semisweet chocolate

pecans

1 Put the butter and chocolate in a bowl and stand it over a saucepan of hot, but not boiling water. Make sure the water doesn't touch the bowl. Leave until they have both melted and then stir them together.

2 Stir the sugar into the butter and chocolate mixture and leave for a while to cool slightly.

3 Cut a piece of wax paper to fit the bottom of a 7in square cake pan.

4 Preheat the oven to 350°F. Beat the eggs into the chocolate mixture, then stir in the flour and nuts.

5 Pour the mixture into the lined cake pan and smooth the top. Cook for 25–35 minutes, until firm around the edges but still slightly soft in the middle.

6 Cut into nine squares and let cool in the pan. Dredge the brownies with a little confectioner's sugar and serve hot or cold.

Bacon Twists

Making bread is always fun, so try this tasty version and add that extra twist to your breakfast. Serve with soft cheese with herbs.

Makes 12

INGREDIENTS
4 cups all-purpose flour
1 envelope rapid-rise yeast
½ tsp salt
1¾ cups hand-hot water
12 strips lean bacon
1 egg, beaten

water   *flour*   *egg*

yeast

salt

bacon

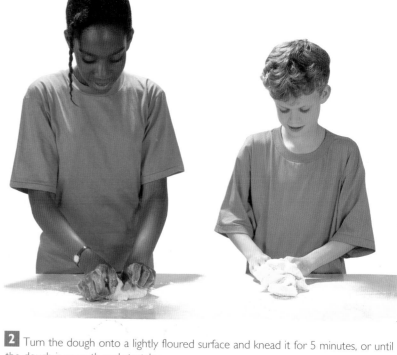

1 Mix the flour, yeast and salt in a bowl and stir them together. Add a little of the water and mix with a knife. Add the remaining water and use your hands to pull the mixture together, to make a sticky dough.

2 Turn the dough onto a lightly floured surface and knead it for 5 minutes, or until the dough is smooth and stretchy.

3 Divide into 12 pieces and roll each one into a sausage shape.

4 Lay each strip of bacon on a chopping board and run the back of the knife down its length, to stretch it slightly. Wind a strip of bacon around each dough "sausage."

5 Brush the "sausages" with beaten egg and arrange them on a lightly oiled baking sheet. Put somewhere warm for 30 minutes, or until they have doubled in size. Preheat the oven to 400°F and cook the "sausages" for 20–25 minutes, until cooked and browned.

COOK'S TIP
This same basic dough mix can be used to make rolls or a loaf of bread. Tap the base of the breadstick – if it sounds hollow, it's cooked.

Gingerbread Jungle

Snappy cookies in animal shapes, which can be decorated in your own style.

Makes 14

INGREDIENTS
1½ cups self-rising flour
½ tsp baking soda
½ tsp ground cinnamon
2 tsp sugar
4 tbsp butter or margarine
3 tbsp corn syrup
oil, for baking sheets
½ cup confectioner's sugar
1–2 tsp water

flour

confectioner's sugar

corn syrup

butter

sugar

cinnamon

baking soda

1 Preheat the oven to 375°F. Put the flour, baking soda, cinnamon and sugar in a bowl and mix together. Melt the butter or margarine and corn syrup in a saucepan. Pour this mixture over the dry ingredients.

2 Mix together well and then use your hands to pull the mixture together to make a dough.

3 Turn onto a lightly floured surface and roll out to a ¼in thickness.

4 Use animal cutters to cut shapes from the dough and arrange them on two lightly oiled baking sheets, leaving enough room between them to rise. Press the trimmings back into a ball, roll it out and cut more shapes. Continue until the dough is used up. Cook for 8–12 minutes, until lightly browned.

5 Let the cookies cool slightly, before lifting them onto a wire rack with a metal spatula. Sift the confectioner's sugar into a small bowl and add enough water to make a fairly soft icing. Put the icing in a pastry bag fitted with a small, plain nozzle and pipe decorations on the cookies.

COOK'S TIP
Any cutters can be used with the same mixture. Obviously the smaller the cutters, the more cookies you will make.

Blueberry Muffins

Monster muffins that contain whole fresh blueberries that burst in the mouth when bitten.

Makes 9

INGREDIENTS
3¼ cups all-purpose flour
⅞ cup sugar
1½ tbsp baking powder
¾ cup butter, coarsely chopped
1 egg, beaten
1 egg yolk
⅔ cup milk
grated rind of 1 lemon
1½ cups fresh blueberries

milk *sugar*

flour *baking powder*

egg

egg yolk

lemon *blueberries*

butter

1 Preheat the oven to 400°F. Line a muffin pan with nine large paper muffin cups.

3 In a separate bowl, beat the egg, egg yolk, milk and lemon rind together.

2 Put the flour, sugar, baking powder and butter in a bowl. Use your fingertips to work the butter into the flour, until the mixture looks like breadcrumbs.

4 Pour the egg and milk mixture into the flour mixture, add the blueberries and mix gently together.

5 Divide the mixture among the muffin cups and cook for 30–40 minutes, until they are risen and brown.

6 Push a skewer into the middle of one of the muffins. The muffins are cooked if it comes out clean. Lift onto a wire rack to cool.

COOK'S TIP
As the muffins have fresh fruit in them, they will not keep for longer than four days, so best eat them immediately!

Chunky Choc Bars

A no-cook cake that's a smash-hit with everyone.

Makes 12

INGREDIENTS
12 oz semisweet chocolate
½ cup butter
15 oz can condensed milk
8 oz whole wheat cookies,
  broken
⅓ cup raisins
4 oz ready-to-eat dried peaches,
  coarsely chopped
½ cup hazelnuts or pecans,
  coarsely chopped

condensed milk

whole wheat cookies

hazelnuts

butter

semisweet chocolate

dried peaches

raisins

1 Line a 7 × 11in cake pan with plastic wrap.

2 Put the chocolate and butter in a large bowl over a pan of hot but not boiling water (the bowl must not touch the water) and let melt. Stir until well mixed.

3 Beat the condensed milk into the chocolate and butter mixture.

4 Add the cookies, raisins, peaches and nuts and mix well, until all the ingredients are coated in chocolate.

5 Turn the mixture into the prepared pan, making sure it is pressed well into the corners. Leave the top craggy. Put in the fridge and leave to set.

6 Lift the cake out of the pan using the plastic wrap and then peel it off. Cut into 12 bars and keep chilled – until you are ready to eat it!

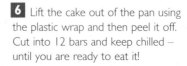

Peanut Cookies

Packing up a picnic? Got a birthday party coming up? Make sure some of these nutty cookies are on the menu.

Makes 25

INGREDIENTS
1 cup butter
2 tbsp smooth peanut butter
1 cup confectioner's sugar
scant ½ cup cornstarch
2 cups all-purpose flour
1 cup unsalted peanuts

flour

cornstarch

peanut butter

butter

unsalted peanuts

confectioner's sugar

1 Put the butter and peanut butter in a bowl and beat together. Add the confectioner's sugar, cornstarch and flour and mix together with your hands, to make a soft dough.

2 Preheat the oven to 350°F and lightly oil two baking sheets. Roll the mixture into 25 small balls, using floured hands, and place the balls on the two baking sheets. Leave plenty of room for the cookies to spread.

3 Press the tops of the balls of dough flat, using either the back of a fork or your fingertips.

4 Press some of the peanuts into each of the cookies. Cook for 15–20 minutes, until lightly browned. Let the cookies cool for a few minutes before lifting them carefully onto a wire rack with a metal spatula. When they are cool, pack them in a tin.

COOK'S TIP
Make really monster cookies by making bigger balls of dough. Leave plenty of room on the baking sheets for them to spread, though.

Five-Spice Fingers

Light, crumbly cookies with an unusual Chinese five-spice flavoring.

Makes 28

INGREDIENTS
½ cup margarine
½ cup confectioner's sugar
1 cup all-purpose flour
2 tsp five-spice powder
oil, for greasing
grated rind and juice of
   ½ orange

orange

confectioner's sugar

five-spice powder

margarine

flour

1 Put the margarine and half the confectioner's sugar in a bowl and beat with a wooden spoon, until the mixture is smooth, creamy and soft.

2 Add the flour and five-spice powder and beat again. Put the mixture in a large pastry bag fitted with a large star nozzle.

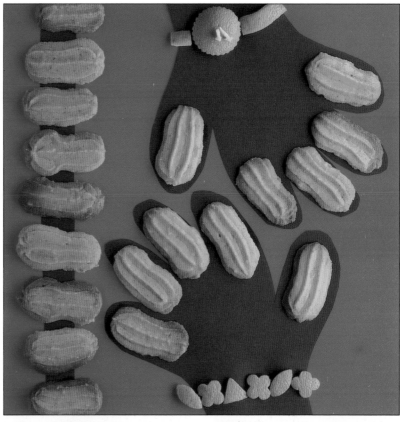

3 Preheat the oven to 350°F. Lightly grease two baking sheets and pipe short lines of mixture, about 3in long, on them. Leave enough room for them to spread. Cook for 15 minutes, until lightly browned. Let cool slightly, before lifting them onto a wire rack with a metal spatula.

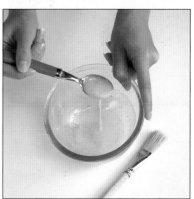

4 Sift the remaining confectioner's sugar into a small bowl and stir in the orange rind. Add enough juice to make a thin icing and brush it over the cookies while they are still warm.

COOK'S TIP
Delicious served with ice cream or creamy desserts.

Carrot Cake

This is full of healthy fiber – yet moist and soft at the same time.

Serves 10 – 12

INGREDIENTS
2 cups self-rising flour
2 tsp baking powder
1 scant cup brown sugar
4 oz ready-to-eat dried figs,
  coarsely chopped
8 oz carrots, grated
2 small ripe bananas, mashed
2 eggs
⅔ cup sunflower oil
¾ cup cream cheese
1½ cups confectioner's sugar,
  sifted
small colored candies, nuts or
  grated chocolate, to decorate

sunflower oil
dried figs
cream cheese
self-rising flour
baking powder
confectioner's sugar
eggs
carrots
bananas
brown sugar

1 Lightly grease a 7in round spring-form cake pan with a removable rim. Cut a piece of wax paper to fit the bottom of the pan.

2 Preheat the oven to 350°F. Put the flour, baking powder and sugar into a large bowl and mix well. Stir in the figs.

3 Using your hands, squeeze as much liquid out of the grated carrots as you can and add them to the bowl. Mix in the mashed bananas.

4 Beat the eggs and oil together and pour them into the mixture. Beat together with a wooden spoon.

5 Spoon into the prepared pan and smooth the top. Cook for 1 – 1¼ hours, until a skewer pushed into the center of the cake comes out clean. Remove the cake from the pan and let cool on a wire rack.

6 Beat the cream cheese and confectioner's sugar together, to make a thick icing. Spread it over the top of the cake. Decorate with small colored candies, nuts or grated chocolate. Cut in small wedges, to serve.

COOK'S TIP
Because this cake contains moist vegetables and fruit, it will not keep longer than a week, but you probably won't find this a problem!

Lemon Meringue Cupcakes

Turn a favorite pie into cupcakes – soft lemon sponge topped with crisp meringue.

Makes 18

INGREDIENTS
½ cup margarine
scant 1 cup sugar
2 eggs
1 cup self-rising flour
1 tsp baking powder
grated rind of 2 lemons
2 tbsp lemon juice
2 egg whites

flour

sugar

lemon juice

baking powder

eggs

lemons

margarine

2 Beat in the eggs, flour, baking powder, half the lemon rind and all the lemon juice.

3 Stand 18 small paper cups in two muffin pans , and divide the mixture between them.

1 Preheat the oven to 375°F. Put the margarine in a bowl and beat until soft. Add ½ cup of the sugar and continue to beat until the mixture is smooth and creamy.

4 Beat the egg whites in a clean bowl, until they stand in soft peaks.

5 Stir in the remaining sugar and lemon rind.

COOK'S TIP

Make sure that you whisk the egg whites enough before adding the sugar – when you lift out the whisk they should stand in peaks that just flop over slightly at the top.
Use a mixture of oranges and lemons, for a sweeter taste.

6 Put a spoonful of the meringue mixture on each cupcake. Cook for 20–25 minutes, until the meringue is crisp and brown. Serve hot or cold.

Citrus Punch & Spicy Nuts

A sizzler of a cold drink for hot days, served with spicy nuts.

Serves 4

INGREDIENTS
FOR THE CITRUS PUNCH
juice of 2 pink grapefruit
juice of 2 lemons
juice of 4 oranges
⅔ cup pineapple juice
2 tbsp sugar
2½ cups lemonade
slices of lime and orange,
   to decorate

FOR THE SPICY NUTS
6 tbsp butter
1 tbsp oil
2 garlic cloves, crushed
2 tbsp Worcestershire sauce
1 tsp chili powder
1 tsp ground turmeric
1 tsp cayenne pepper
4 cups mixed nuts

1 To make the citrus punch, put the fruit juices in a large pitcher or bowl, stir in the sugar, then chill.

2 Add the lemonade and fruit slices, just before serving.

pink grapefruit

lemonade

pineapple juice

oranges

lemons

garlic

oil

Worcestershire sauce

butter

turmeric

chili powder

cayenne pepper

sugar

mixed nuts

3 Make the nuts while the punch is chilling. Heat the butter and oil in a frying pan until the butter melts. Stir in the garlic, Worcestershire sauce, spices and seasonings.

4 Cook gently for 1 minute, stirring all the time, then add the nuts and cook for 4–5 minutes, until lightly browned. Drain on kitchen towels and let cool before serving with the punch.

Mock Mimosa & Twizzles

Impress the grown-ups with your own knockout of a drink, which will flatten the real thing. Serve with herby cheese twizzles.

Serves 6–8

INGREDIENTS
FOR THE MOCK MIMOSA
2½ cups fresh orange juice
3 tbsp lemon juice
½ cup confectioner's sugar, sifted
1¼ cups natural lemon soda, or use your favorite, chilled
orange slices, to decorate

FOR THE TWIZZLES
2 cups all-purpose flour
½ cup butter, coarsely chopped
1 tbsp dried mixed herbs
2 oz aged Cheddar cheese, grated
cold water, to mix
salt and pepper

lemon soda

flour   *butter*

orange slices   *water*   *cheese*

orange juice   *pepper*

mixed herbs   *confectioner's sugar*

 lemon juice

1 For the mock mimosa, mix the orange and lemon juice and the confectioner's sugar in a pitcher, stir and chill.

2 Just before serving, add the lemon soda and decorate the pitcher or the glasses with orange slices.

COOK'S TIP
Make some of the pastry strips into circles. After baking, slip three pastry strips inside each circle so each guests gets his or her personal set of twizzles.

3 Make the twizzles while the drink is chilling. Preheat the oven to 375°F. Put the flour and the butter in a bowl. Work in the butter, then stir in the herbs, grated cheese and seasoning and add enough water to be able to pull the pastry together and knead it into a firm but not sticky dough.

4 Roll out the dough until it is ⅛in thick and cut it into 6in strips, about ⅓in wide. Twist each strip once or twice and arrange them in rows on a greased baking sheet. Cook for 15–20 minutes, until golden brown. Cool the twizzles on a wire rack.

Hot Chocolate & Choc-tipped Cookies

Get those cold hands wrapped around a steaming hot drink, and tuck into choc-tipped cookies.

Serves 2

INGREDIENTS

FOR THE HOT CHOCOLATE
6 tbsp drinking chocolate powder, plus a little extra for sprinkling
2 tbsp sugar, or more according to taste
2½ cups milk
2 large squirts aerosol cream (optional)

FOR THE CHOC-TIPPED COOKIES
½ cup soft margarine
3 tbsp confectioner's sugar, sifted
1¼ cups all-purpose flour
few drops of vanilla extract
3 oz semisweet chocolate

  soft margarine

milk

  vanilla extract

sugar

  aerosol cream

drinking chocolate powder

 flour

confectioner's sugar

 *semisweet chocolate*

1 To make the drinking chocolate, put the drinking chocolate powder and the sugar in a saucepan. Add the milk and bring it to a boil, whisking all the time. Divide between two mugs. Add more sugar if needed. Top with a squirt of cream, if you like.

2 To make the choc-tipped cookies, put the margarine and confectioner's sugar in a bowl and beat them together until very soft. Mix in the flour and vanilla extract. Preheat the oven to 350°F and lightly grease two large baking sheets.

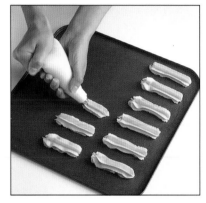

3 Put the mixture in a large pastry bag fitted with a large star nozzle and pipe 4–5in lines on the baking sheets. Cook for 15–20 minutes, until pale golden brown. Allow to cool slightly before lifting onto a wire rack. Let the cookies cool completely.

4 Put the chocolate in a small bowl. Stand in a pan of hot, but not boiling, water and let melt. Dip both ends of each cookie in the chocolate, put back on the rack and let set.

COOK'S TIP
Make round cookies if you prefer, and dip half of each cookie in melted chocolate.

Fruit Crush & Fruit Kebabs

Fruit crush is just the ticket on a sultry summer's day, served with mouthwatering fruit kebabs.

Serves 6

INGREDIENTS
FOR THE FRUIT CRUSH
1¼ cups orange juice
1¼ cups pineapple juice
1¼ cups tropical fruit juice
2 cups lemonade
fresh pineapple slices and
    fresh cherries, to decorate

FOR THE FRUIT KEBABS
24 small strawberries
24 green seedless grapes
12 marshmallows
1 kiwi fruit, peeled and cut in
    12 wedges
1 banana
1 tbsp lemon juice

1 To make the fruit crush, put the orange juice and the pineapple juice into ice cube trays and freeze them until solid.

2 Mix together the tropical fruit juice and lemonade in a large pitcher. Put a mixture of the ice cubes in each glass and pour the fruit crush over. Decorate the glasses with the pineapple slices and cherries.

3 To make the fruit kebabs, thread 2 strawberries, 2 grapes, a marshmallow and a wedge of kiwi fruit onto each of twelve wooden skewers.

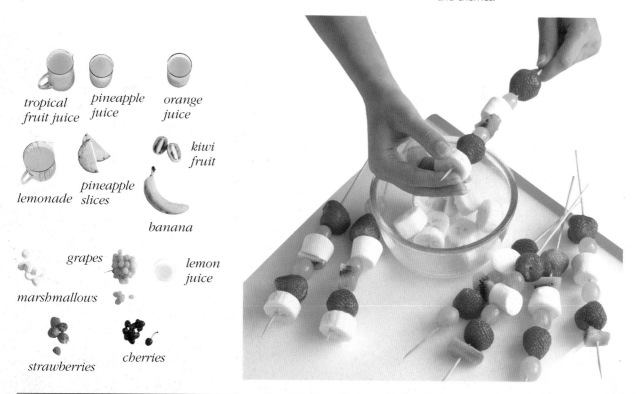

tropical fruit juice *pineapple juice* *orange juice*

lemonade *pineapple slices* *kiwi fruit*

banana

grapes *lemon juice*

marshmallows

strawberries *cherries*

4 Peel the banana and cut it into twelve slices. Toss it in the lemon juice and thread on to the skewers. Serve immediately.

Strawberry Smoothie & Stars-in-your-Eyes Cookies

A real smoothie that's lip-smackingly special, when served with crunchy stars-in-your-eyes cookies.

Serves 4–6

INGREDIENTS
FOR THE STRAWBERRY SMOOTHIE
2 cups strawberries
⅔ cup strained plain yogurt
2 cups ice-cold milk
2 tbsp confectioner's sugar

FOR STARS-IN-YOUR-EYES COOKIES
½ cup butter
1½ cups all-purpose flour
¼ cup sugar
2 tbsp corn syrup
2 tbsp preserving sugar

milk

flour

plain yogurt

confectioner's sugar

corn syrup

strawberries

preserving sugar

sugar

butter

1 To make the stars-in-your-eyes cookies, put the butter, flour and sugar in a bowl and work in the fat with your fingertips, until the mixture looks like breadcrumbs. Stir in the sugar and then knead together to make a ball. Chill in the fridge for 30 minutes.

2 Preheat the oven to 350°F and lightly grease two baking sheets. Roll out the dough on a floured surface to a ¼in thickness and use a 3in star-shaped cutter to stamp out the cookies.

3 Arrange the cookies on a baking sheet, leaving enough room for them to rise. Press the trimmings together and keep rolling out and cutting more cookies until all the mixture has been used. Bake for 10–15 minutes, until they are golden brown.

4 Put the syrup in a small microwave-safe bowl and heat it on HIGH for 12 seconds or heat for 1–2 minutes over simmering water. Brush over the cookies while they are still warm. Sprinkle a little preserving sugar on top of each one and let cool.

5 To make the strawberry smoothies, reserve a few of the strawberries for decoration and put the rest in a food processor or blender with the yogurt. Process until fairly smooth.

6 Add the milk and confectioner's sugar, process again and pour into glasses. Serve each glass decorated with one or two of the reserved strawberries.

INDEX

A

Apples: lazy apple t
  turnover, 64

B

Bacon: bacon twists, 74
  chicken chips, 43
  turkey surprise packages, 54
Baking, 14
Barbecue, 14
Beef: homeburgers, 52
Blenders, 10
Blueberry muffins, 78
Boiled rice, 20
Boiling, 14
Bread: bacon twists, 74
  tasty toasts, 30
Broiled peaches, 65
Brownies, 72
Butterscotch: ice cream
  bombes, 70

C

Cabbage: chunky veggy
  salad, 36
Cakes: carrot cake, 84
  chunky choc bars, 80
  lemon meringue
    cupcakes, 86
Carrots: carrot cake, 84
  chunky veggy salad, 36
  preparing, 16
  see-in-the-dark soup, 28
Cashews: yellow
  chicken, 37
Cheese: broiled
    peaches, 65
  cheese snacks, 89
  chili cheese nachos, 31
  homeburgers, 52
  pancake packages, 40
  Popeye's pie, 53
  raving ravioli, 50
  tasty toasts, 30
  twizzles, 89
Cheesecake: summer fruit
  cheesecake, 66
Cherry tomato pizza, 49
Chicken: chicken chips, 43
  cock-a-noodle soup, 27
  nutty chicken kebabs, 25
  sticky fingers, 46
  yellow chicken, 37
Chili: chili cheese nachos, 31
Chips: chicken chips, 43
Chocolate: brownies, 72
  chocolate cups, 68

chocolate cream puffs, 60
  choc-tipped cookies, 90
  chunky choc bars, 80
  hot chocolate, 90
  ice cream bombes, 70
  puffy pears, 71
Chopping boards, 10
Chunky choc bars, 80
Chunky veggy salad, 36
Citrus punch, 88
Cock-a-noodle soup, 27
Cookies: choc-tipped
    cookies, 90
  five-spice fingers, 83
  gingerbread jungle, 76
  stars-in-your-eyes
    cookies, 94
Cooking terms, 14, 15
Cream, whipping, 19

D

Drinks: citrus punch, 89
  fruit crush, 92
  hot chocolate, 90
  mock mimosa 89
  strawberry smoothies, 94

E

Eggplant: eggs in a
    blanket, 42
  give 'em a roasting, 34
Eggs: eggs in a blanket, 42
  separating, 18
  wicked tortilla
    wedges, 32
Equipment, 9, 10, 12

F

Fennel: turkey surprise
    packages, 54
Filo pastry: Popeye's
    pie, 53
Fish 'n' rice, 56
Five-spice fingers, 83
Fruit: citrus punch, 88
  fruit crush, 92
  fruit kebabs, 92
  let's get tropical, 61
  monster meringues, 62
  summer fruit
    cheesecake, 66

G

Garnish, 14
Ginger: fresh, grating, 17
Gingerbread jungle, 76
Grating, 17, 18

H

Ham: pancake packages, 40
Herbs: tiny toads, 48
Homeburgers, 52
Honey chops, 57

I

Ice cream bombes, 70

K

Kebabs: nutty chicken
    kebabs, 25
Kitchen, safety in, 8, 9, 10
Kneading, 14
Knives, 12

L

Lamb: party lamb, 58
Lazy apple turnover, 64
Lemons: citrus punch, 88
  juice, squeezing, 17
  lemon meringue
    cupcakes, 86
  rind, grating, 17
  squeezer, 12
Let's get tropical, 61

M

Marinade, 14
Mashed potatoes, 20
Measuring equipment, 10
Meringues: lemon meringue
    cupcakes, 86
  monster meringues, 62
Microwave ovens, 9
Mock mimosa, 89
Monster meringues, 62·
Muffins: blueberry
    muffins, 78
Mushrooms: chunky veggy
    salad, 36
  give 'em a roasting, 34
  pile-it-high mushrooms, 24

N

Noodles: cock-a-noodle
    soup, 27
Nuts: brownies, 72
  chunky choc bars, 80
  lazy apple turnover, 64
  spicy nuts, 88
Nutty chicken kebabs, 25

O

Onions: onion gravy, 48
  preparing, 16
Oven safety, 9

P

Pancake packages, 40
Pans, 10, 14, 19
Party lamb, 58
Pasta, 21
  chicken chips, 43
  pepperoni pasta, 38
  raving ravioli, 50
Pastry brush, 12
Pastry wheel, 12
Peaches: broiled peaches, 65
  let's get tropical, 61
Peanut butter: nutty chicken
    kebabs, 25
  peanut cookies, 82
Pears: puffy pears, 71
Pepperoni pasta, 38
Peppers: cherry tomato
    pizza, 49
  eggs in a blanket, 42
  give 'em a roasting, 34
  tasty toasts, 30
Pile-it-high mushrooms, 24
Piping, 14
  bags and nozzles, 12
Poaching, 15
Popeye's pie, 53
Pork: honey chops, 57
  sticky fingers, 46
Potatoes: mashed potatoes, 20
  peeler, 12
  roast potatoes, 58
  skinny dips, 22
  something very fishy, 44
  sticky fingers, 46
  wicked tortilla wedges, 32
Puffy pears, 71
Purée, 15

R

Raspberries: summer fruit
    cheesecake, 66
Raving ravioli, 50
Rice: boiled rice, 20
  fish 'n' rice, 56
Roast potatoes, 58
Rolling pin, 12
Roux, 15

S

Salad: chunky veggy salad, 36
Salad dressing, 21
Salmon: something very
    fishy, 44
Sausages: tiny toads, 48
Seafood: fish 'n' rice, 56
Seasoning, 15

See-in-the-dark soup, 28
Shrimp: fish 'n' rice, 56
Simmering, 15
Skinny dips, 22
Small tools, 12
Something very fishy, 44
Soup: cock-a-noodle soup, 27
  see-in-the-dark soup, 28
  super bowl soup, 26
Spare ribs: sticky fingers, 46
Spicy nuts, 88
Spinach: Popeye's pie, 53
  raving ravioli, 50
Sticky fingers, 46
Stir-fry, 15
Stoves, 9
Strawberries: summer fruit
    cheesecake, 66
  strawberry smoothies, 94
Summer fruit cheesecake, 66
Super bowl soup, 26

T

Tasty toasts, 30
Timers, 9
Tiny toads, 48
Tomatoes: cherry tomato
    pizza, 49
  give 'em a roasting, 34
Tongs, 12
Tools, 10, 12
Tortilla chips: chili cheese
    nachos, 31
Trout: raving ravioli, 50
Turkey surprise packages, 54
Twizzles, 89

V

Vegetables: chunky veggy
    salad, 36
  give 'em a roasting, 34
  super bowl soup, 26

W

Whisks, 10, 12
Wicked tortilla wedges, 32
Wooden spoons, 12

Y

Yellow chicken, 37

Z

Zester, 12
Zucchini: eggs in a blanket, 42
  give 'em a roasting, 34